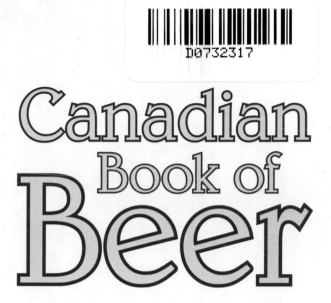

Canadian Book of Beer

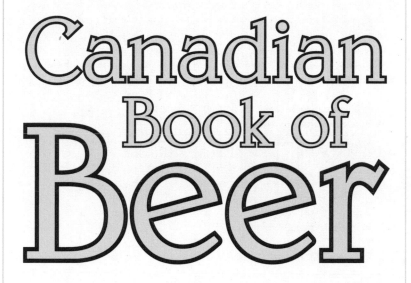

Canadian
Book of
Beer

Steve Cameron

BLUE
BIKE
BOOKS

The Publisher: Blue Bike Books
Website: www.bluebikebooks.com

Library and Archives Canada Cataloguing in Publication

Cameron, Steve, 1981–
     Canadian book of beer / by Steve Cameron.

Includes bibliographical references.

ISBN 978-1-897278-64-2

     1. Beer—Canada—Miscellanea. 2. Beer industry—Canada—History. I. Title.
TP573.C3C34 2009   641.2'30971   C2009-900186-1

Project Director: Nicholle Carrière
Project Editor: Carla MacKay
Cover Image: Courtesy of Dreamstime; © Mist | Dreamstime.com
Photos: Courtesy of Dreamstime and Photos.com
Illustrator: Djordje Todorovic, Peter Tyler and Roger Garcia

We acknowledge the support of the Alberta Foundation for the Arts for our publishing program.

We acknowledge the financial support of the Government of Canada through the Book Publishing Industry Development Program (BPIDP) for our publishing activities.

PC: 1

DEDICATION

To all those I consider family—biological and extended—who have provided support over the years, and specifically to Claudine—I couldn't have done it without you, baby.

CONTENTS

ACKNOWLEDGMENTS

Aside from beer, an old school pal, editor Carla MacKay, deserves the biggest thanks. Without her, this project wouldn't have happened—nor would it read so well. Thanks for thinking of me, Carla.

I'd also like to thank Michael Worek, to whom I owe 90 percent of my publishing success; thanks, Michael, for the constant support and advice.

Thanks to all those who lent a hand with the brainstorming and research for this book. And a huge thanks goes out to chef Howard Dubrovsky, the founder of Food Cult, who took time out of his busy schedule to help create some delicious beer recipes—and who also now swears the only pancakes he'll eat are pancakes made with beer! Howard's impressive culinary skills are featured on his website, www.howard-dubrovsky.com.

With the writing of this book, I suppose I have joined a fraternity of writers who have dedicated many long hours to the world of beer. I'm honoured to have my work stand alongside theirs. Specifically, I'd like to note the work of Stephen Beaumont and Allen Winn Sneath, both whose dedication to the Canadian beer industry is something all Canadian beer drinkers should raise a glass to.

Lastly, thanks to all those I've shared a pint with over the years, and to my go-to beer-drinking guys, Jay, Djordje and Dan. Also to Joe Gibbons, who unfortunately admitted to me that he likes Coors Light, but nonetheless shared my first beer experience.

INTRODUCTION

My first beer was an American lager called Mickey's. It was a 5.6-percent alcohol-by-volume beer, packaged in a green, keg-shaped, squat 350-millilitre bottle with a short neck and an extra-wide mouth sealed with a screw cap. The cap even had an illustration of a bee on the top. The only thing typical about this first brew experience was that it came from the fridge of a parent, my friend Joe's dad.

At the time, Joe and I were 15 or 16 years old, and neither of us had ever tried beer. Our teenage taste buds were accustomed to the sweet, sugary goodness of pop and juice, so the first alcoholic drink we readily consumed was vodka and orange juice—it seemed a no-brainer. But, for me at least, there was a latent desire to try beer. Whether it was the stereotypes portrayed in movies such as *Porky's, Ski School, Revenge of the Nerds* and *Animal House*, or the commercials aired by Molson and Labatt that cleverly catered to teenage mores—or that my dad drank beer—my mind was of the opinion that beer was what men drank, so I'd better get drinking it too.

Joe and I each grabbed a Mickey's wide-mouthed beer and headed to the sink. The idea was to just chug it and get it over with. Then we'd be beer drinkers, we thought. As weak-tasting as I'm sure Mickey's beer is to a seasoned beer drinker, the little hop and malt profiles that were present hit our teenage palates and we reacted violently to the bitter, carbonated, acrid sensation in our mouths. Both of us immediately spit up the beer and dumped the rest down the drain. End of experiment.

But I was still hooked on the idea that beer was what I was *supposed* to drink. I continued trying it, and then hating it, until I discovered a malt-based beverage made with lemon flavour:

Boomerang. It was like beer but had the sweetness I was familiar with. Boomerang was my gateway to the world of beer.

Once I was able to fully stomach a few different brews (and by these I mean North American lagers), I, as so many other teenagers, thought I should quickly associate myself with a brand—an identity in the beer world that labelled me as belonging to a certain camp and set me apart from the hoards of other beer drinkers. But if only this were true! My "associations" changed several times as I developed a sense of taste and smell for beer. The first brand to hold my allegiance was Molson Canadian, which quickly turned to Moosehead, then to Brick's Red Cap. It was during the formative years of university that I first started to learn about beer and really develop a taste for what the craft brewers of Ontario were making. Since then, I haven't been able to get enough!

I think the following theory is typical of many Canadian beer-drinkers: no matter what your age, the craft-brew renaissance that was kick-started in 1982 on Canada's West Coast in Victoria has most likely come to inform your beer tastes and beer-buying decisions. In the late 1970s and early 1980s, Canadians had a scant choice between three major breweries: Molson, Labatt and Carling O'Keefe, all of which had a handful of national and regional brands (each more or less the same), and a few regional breweries, like Moosehead in New Brunswick and Sick's Lethbridge Brewery in Alberta. These regional breweries provided an alternative to the Big Three but hardly offered something different. So the other choice for Canadians was imported beer. Many of these options (save for Guinness), however, were close to what was already being consumed in Canada: golden lagers and unchallenging ales.

Today, craft beer is produced in every province, and, across the country, drinkers can find a craft brew to satisfy any taste.

You like your beer hoppy? Try Victoria's Phillips Brewing and their award-winning Amnesiac double India Pale Ale. You want a full-bodied Scotch ale? Try the Pump House Scotch Ale from New Brunswick. How about something truly different? Try Ontario's Great Lakes Brewery and their Green Tea Ale.

Fortunately (or unfortunately, depending on how you look at it), craft beer is still considered a specialty market. When Prohibition was lifted and provincial agencies were created to oversee the importation, distribution, buying and selling of all alcohol, it was mandated that in order to sell beer in a specific province, the beer also had to be produced in that province. In the beginning, this system created a wide array of breweries that made beer for regional tastes. It also meant that the Big Guys, if they wanted a true national brand, had to have a brewery in every province—hence the period of massive buyouts sparked by E.P. Taylor between the 1930s and 1970s. When NAFTA was passed in 1994, trade regulations began to loosen trade between provinces, but for the beverage-alcohol industry, the doors weren't (and aren't) yet wide open: brewers who sell beer outside of their province of manufacture are subject to levies enforced by the provincial liquor commissions and agencies to which they are importing. The exception is Alberta, whose borders are pretty much free of red tape, given that the province's liquor industry became private in 1993.

With the rise of the craft segment and the cost of exporting beer to other provinces, consumers are now offered regional-based products that more accurately reflect the tastes of their area. For instance, in Ontario, tastes lean toward European/German-style lagers and English-style ales, whereas Québec tends to favour fruity, complex, strong Belgian-style ales and lagers. The downside to all of this, of course, is that if you want to try a brew from Halifax, you more than likely have to go to Halifax to get it. The upside is that craft brewers are dedicating themselves to the art of making beer—taking the time to produce small batches with quality ingredients. In turn, craft brewers don't need to worry about trying to satisfy the tastes of an entire country (three national breweries already spend copious amounts of money doing that), and they can be active community participants, giving something back to the people to which they owe their livelihood.

Canada's craft-brew renaissance is the most recent development in what is a long, proud, inventive and zany history of Canadian brewing. When John Molson founded his brewery in 1786, he had no idea that he would lead a brewing revolution or that his brewery would become the oldest beer brand and brewery in North America; when Labatt launched the twist-off cap on a long-neck bottle in 1984, the brewer didn't imagine it would set the stage for the new Industry Standard Bottle while also creating a Canadian icon out of the stubby, which they effectively killed. And when John Mitchell opened the Horseshoe Bay Brewery on Victoria Island in 1982, he didn't realize the brewing revolution was about to begin.

Throughout all of these changes, the Canadian brewing industry endured war, Depression and Prohibition while shaping the taste of discerning drinkers countrywide. It is my hope that not only will this book provide insight into who and what has made Canada's beer industry what it is today, but that it will also explain what beer is, where it comes from and what styles you might find down at your local pub. The *Canadian Book of Beer* also teaches how to pair beer and food, how to cook with beer and, most importantly, how to go from having no beer at all to getting it, opening it, pouring it, tasting it, storing it and returning those empties.

Beer is a pastime and a passion, and, as I figured out, is not just what my dad drank. It's more than a beverage; beer is an integral part of the social fabric of this nation. So indulge, as so many Canadians do, with a great Canadian beer, and enjoy a little light reading—and when you're finished, I suggest reaching for another cold one.

Cheers!

THE FOUR MAGIC INGREDIENTS

Walk to the Sink

If there is one commonality between beer and your body (that has nothing to do with a six-pack), it is that both beer and your body are mostly comprised of water. So important is water to the beer industry that older breweries were typically constructed near a natural water source. Beer is close to 90 percent water in its makeup, and the thought was that if the beverage contained so much water, it just seemed wise to have some nearby. As breweries began to develop on a larger scale, a clean, reliable water source was of the utmost importance. The end result of what was originally done out of convenience is, as we now know, that water shapes the taste and feel of a beer. In fact, within pioneering beer communities such as Pilsen, Czech Republic (where Pilsner was invented and where they use soft water), and Burton-on-Trent, England (where they use mineral-filled water and produce what many consider the best pale ales in the world), the standard has been set for style. So respected is this water treatment that ale brewers the world over "Burtonize" their water (treat their water to replicate Burton's mineral content).

It generally follows that softer water is used for lagers and harder water for ales. The more minerals in the water, the more opportunity for unique and interesting combinations of flavour as the minerals influence the grain and hops. Therefore, lagers, made with softer water, are usually crisp, easy-drinking affairs, while ales, made with harder water, are normally more complex and robust in their taste, in part because the water used contains more minerals. For example, Neustadt Springs Brewery in Neustadt, Ontario, operates in the province's oldest active brewery (built in 1859) and has a natural spring that runs in caverns directly beneath it. According to brewmaster Andy Stimpson, the water at Neustadt is very close to Burton-on-Trent's mineral content and works marvelously well with Neustadt's line of ales and full-flavoured lagers. On the other hand, the Quidi Vidi Brewing Company in Newfoundland uses 12,000-year-old iceberg water—with no organic or mineral compounds—to create its clean, crisp, drinkable Iceberg lager.

Grain on the Brain

Grain is to beer what the grape is to wine. It's as simple as that. Without grain, the production of beer is not possible. Yeast ferments the sugars from grain to create alcohol, so if you have grain, you can make beer. Even rice can be used to make beer— just ask the Japanese. Although sake is often called rice wine, it is a misnomer, as the production of sake/rice wine is really the process of creating beer. Corn, too, is often used in the production of beer; for example, in Budweiser. Cheaper than barley, corn is typically used in discount lagers as a cost-cutting measure. Corn also provides brewers with a finished product that is both light in colour and taste, something big brewers advertise as being desirable. In the beer trade, corn, and any other low-cost substitute that doesn't enhance the brew in a style-defining or altering way, is known as an adjunct ingredient. An adjunct taste is a less-than-enviable quality for a beer, so why is Budweiser, the bestselling beer in the world, using corn? I'll let you make your own conclusions, but I can tell you that it will never be a beer I ask for at my local pub.

On the other hand, there's barley. It's the most popular grain in beer production, and Canada grows a lot of it. As beer authority (not pop star) Michael Jackson attests, the best barley grows in the Northern Hemisphere between latitudes 45° and 55°. BC, Alberta and Saskatchewan are world-famous for

their malt-barley production, and Alberta alone produces over one million tonnes of premium malt barley annually. Other popular forms of grain used in beer production are wheat, rye and oat.

DID YOU  KNOW?

The one million tonnes of premium malt barley Alberta produces for beer production is only 20 percent of the total malt-barley production of the entire province. The remaining 80 percent doesn't pass the rigorous standards malting barley is subject to. What happens to the barley that doesn't make the cut? It gets made into livestock feed.

So What of These Malts
I Keep Hearing About?

Malts are grain. More specifically, malts are malted grain. Often you'll hear brewers using the word "malt" in place of the word "grain." Malting is a process the grain is put through in order to help extract its natural sugars. To do this, grains are soaked and then dried. The amount of time grain is soaked and the method used to dry the grain influences the end colour and flavour of the malt; varieties of finished malts range in colour and taste from dark brown and chocolate-like to blonde and toffee-like.

Not just any grain is malted. In the case of barley, two types of "malting barley" are grown: the two-row and the six-row ("row" refers to the number of rows of barley seeds at the top of the barley stalk). The tops of two-row barley is typically illustrated on beer labels (like the golden stalks at the bottom of the label of Labatt Blue) and beer paraphernalia and because two-row barley yields less malt, the beer containing it can be more expensive. Commonly, two-row is used in ales, and six-row in lagers, but this is not a hard-and-fast rule.

Hop to It

Hops! What can't they do? Back in the 1950s the logic employed by the English brewer Bass was that hops could even put a hop in your step. Bass ads from the era extolled the energy-giving virtues of the hop plant as if it was the Red Bull of today: "They've got tonic powers, they give you energy and vigour, put the life into you when you're tired out."

In reality, it is hard to say that hops contain any of the restorative powers Bass implied. The most vital characteristics the hop plant lends to beer are bitterness, aroma and preservation.

However, it is interesting to note that the hop plant is part of the same botanical family as cannabis—and we are all well aware of the powers of that plant!

Before hops came on to the beer-production scene, brewers used a variety of herbs and spices like rosemary and juniper to spice and preserve their beer. Unfortunately for them, none of their spice varieties worked well or tasted exceptionally good. It was Bavarian monks who paved the way for modern brewing when they discovered that the oils released from the hop plant during the brewing process imparted a bitter flavour that was capable of balancing out the sweetness of the malt. The monks also figured out that hops acted as a good natural preservative.

Hops are still used today for both their flavour-balancing and preservative properties. More than 50 hop varieties are grown for brewing throughout the world. Many of these varieties, like the Saaz and the Cascade, are coveted for their flavour and aroma profiles.

Look to the Yeast

If there is one ingredient to thank for all of those rabble-rousing drunken adventures, horrible pickup lines, awkward trips to

the dance floor and time spent not-so-wisely between the sheets, it is our old friend yeast—a fungus! Yeast is a single-celled micro-organism that exists naturally in the atmosphere. This micro-organism loves sugar and in exchange for it will produce both alcohol and carbon dioxide. Yeast is responsible for making the mixture of water, grain and hops alcoholic. Without yeast, life and history would be a lot less fun.

Just How Old Is Our Old Friend, Yeast?

Yeast has been around the beer game since before beer even had a name. And the funny thing is, beer had a name before yeast did. It took us a long time to figure out what was making our mash of water, barley and spices make us feel so good and tingly. In fact, without microscopes, we were hopeless to identify yeast as something from this world. So, what did we do? We attributed it to God, of course. The chemical reaction yeast caused was believed to happen by divine intervention, so the whole process that transformed our unappetizing watery mush to glorious drink was dubbed "Godisgood."

Thanks again to the industrious, beer-loving Bavarian monks, brewers also know of two types of yeast that are great for making beer: one for making ale, and the other for making lager. Both varieties belong to the *Saccharomyces* species of the genus. The first, a warm-fermenting yeast (read: ale yeast) is called *S. cerevisiae*; the second, a cold-fermenting yeast (read: lager yeast) is called *S. uvarum*. Today, thanks in large part to the studies of Louis Pasteur, brewers are well-versed in the uses of yeast and can make beer from hundreds of isolated yeast strains. Each of these strains falls into one of the two categories: *S. cerevisiae* or *S. uvarum*.

Advanced Tippling

As Jackson says rather cerebrally in his book *Beer*, water and yeast aren't ingredients of the glorious beverage at all; instead, water is the medium of beer production, and yeast is an agent of fermentation. As his logic goes, brewers don't really have a choice as to whether water is an ingredient in beer. Without water, there would be nothing to germinate the grain (to get it ready for fermenting) and therefore no vehicle, or means, for the whole beer-production process. As far as yeast is concerned, fermenting sugar is its natural inclination. Yeast alone doesn't make beer alcoholic, the act of fermentation, which it kick-starts, does—yeast needs to be present for the state change, but for little else.

LAGER VERSUS ALE

The Old Top versus Bottom Debate

When we talk about ale or lager, we are discussing different families of beer, but more than that, we are also talking about their varying processes of fermentation and maturation. Ales and lagers, by and large, go through the same procedure until they hit the fermenting stage. It is here where the style of each beer is truly born.

Once the wort (the water, malt and hop mixture) is ready, it is cooled down, and yeast is added in order to begin the fermentation process. The classic distinction between ale and lager in this process has always been that ales ferment at the top of the barrel while lagers ferment at the bottom. As a general guideline, this still holds credence, but it isn't always true.

What really sets ale and lager apart isn't where the yeast ferments; instead, it is what causes the yeast to ferment in those areas—temperature. Where yeast ferments is a consequence of what temperature the beer is stored at. "Lagern" means "to store" in German, and Bavarian monks discovered their beer turned out differently when they began storing barrels of unfermented wort deep in caves. The monks noticed the reaction that generally happened at the top of their storage vessels (fermenting, which they did not fully understand) began happening toward the bottom of the vessels in colder conditions. The result was a clean, crisp beverage.

What the monks were really witnessing as a result of putting their vats in caves was the activation of yeasts that thrived in colder temperatures and the hibernation of yeasts that needed warmer temperatures to initiate fermentation; or, the activation of lager yeasts and the hibernation of ale yeasts.

Typically, ale yeast works best in moderate temperatures between 15°C and 22°C while lager yeast thrives in cooler temperatures between 6°C and 12°C. Ale is ready to begin maturing after three days of fermenting, while lagers need up to two weeks' fermenting time before they are primed to mature. The maturation of ales and lagers follows a similar timeline to their fermentation times: ales mature more quickly, tending to only need a week or two, while lagers take longer, maturing for a month or more.

The fermentation and maturation process of each different type of yeast for ales and lagers contributes distinct flavours to each brew. The warmer conditions needed for ale yeast to ferment allow the yeast to create esters, which are perceived by the palate as round and fruity: tastes can range from orange to apple to caramel, as well as banana and clove in wheat ales. The colder lagering temperatures inhibit the yeast's ability to produce esters, thus giving lager its classic, clean, crisp finish. And just in case you're wondering, other than an overall haziness from an unfiltered beer, yeast in no way imparts any specific colour profile.

BEER STYLES

All in the Family

When you boil it down, there are really only two families of beer: ale and lager. All the beer styles in the world have their origins traced back to one of these two. Like they say, you can't choose your parents. But what is lovely about ale and lager is that they are incredibly flexible, and over the years people have managed to create many varying offspring, and even those offspring are inspiring new variations on old themes—and hybrids to boot!

You might be surprised at what Canadian brewers are making. Over the following pages you'll find brew styles that are judged every year at the Canadian Brewing Awards, the nation's premier brewing-award event—in 2008, 239 beers were entered from over 50 breweries across the country. For easy reading, I have separated ales, lagers and specialty brews into their own sections. Underneath each sub-style description, the winners of the category for 2007 and 2008 are provided to display the many varieties of beer available across Canada. In judging, the results are traditionally given in medal form, and some categories do not have listings for all three medals. This is because of the scoring thresholds used to decide the winners.

Even though the ale family has more styles than lager, lager is the more popular of the two.

ALE

Barley Wine

Barley wine's name is inspired by the high-alcohol content of the beer, normally between 9 and 12 percent alcohol by volume (ABV). Other than getting better with age, the beer itself has little else in common with wine, although it may, over time, gain a sherry-like aroma. Barley wines have a low hop flavour and, because of their alcohol content, are very malty. Fruit and caramel flavours may be present.

Canadian Brewing Award Winners, 2007
No winners declared

Canadian Brewing Award Winners, 2008
Gold: Barley Wine (2007), Mill Street Brewery, Toronto, Ontario

Silver: Barley Wine, Wild Rose Brewery Ltd., Calgary, Alberta

Bronze: Barley Wine, Pump House Brewery Ltd., Moncton, New Brunswick

Brown Ale

Often made with dark, roasted malts, brown ales frequently have notes of nut, coffee or chocolate. Medium- to dark-brown ales are usually malty affairs with little hopping. A caramel flavour may be present as well, especially when not ice-cold.

Canadian Brewing Award Winners, 2007
Gold: Stonehammer Premium Dark Ale, F&M Brewery, Guelph, Ontario

Silver: Nut Brown Ale, Garrison Brewing Company, Halifax, Nova Scotia

Bronze: Tall Timber Ale, Mt. Begbie Brewing Company, Revelstoke, BC

Canadian Brewing Award Winners, 2008

Gold: Hockley Dark Traditional English Ale, Hockley Valley Brewing, Orangeville, Ontario

Silver: Swans Appleton Brown Ale, Swans Buckerfields Brewery, Victoria, BC

Bronze: First Trax Brown Ale, Fernie Brewing Company, Fernie, BC

Cream Ale

Some would say that cream ale, a North American invention, is a hybrid. The reason for this is because cream ale is made with warm-fermenting ale yeast but is then matured cold, like a lager. The result is a smooth, crisp, light-to-medium hopped brew that sometimes has a slight fruit and malt finish. Generally, cream ales are pale yellow to golden brown in colour.

Canadian Brewing Award Winners, 2007

Gold: True North Cream Ale, Magnotta Brewery, Vaughan, Ontario

Silver: Russell Cream Ale, Russell Brewing Company, Surrey, BC

Bronze: Cameron's Cream Ale, Cameron's Brewing Company, Oakville, Ontario

Canadian Brewing Award Winners, 2008

Gold: Sleeman Cream Ale, Sleeman Brewing, Guelph, Ontario

Silver: Cameron's Cream Ale, Cameron's Brewing Company, Oakville, Ontario

Bronze: True North Cream Ale, Magnotta Brewery, Vaughan, Ontario

English-style Pale Ale (Bitter)

Golden to copper-coloured, this ale gets its name from the higher hopping rates used to achieve sufficient bitterness and subdue the majority of malt flavours. This beer is very fragrant and often contains strong fruit flavours and aromas. When the beer is served at colder temperatures, drinkers may notice some haziness in the liquid.

Canadian Brewing Award Winners, 2007

Gold: Cutthroat Pale Ale, Tree Brewing, Kelowna, BC
Silver: Red Devil Pale Ale, R&B Brewing Company, Vancouver, BC
Bronze: Black Oak Pale Ale, Black Oak Brewing Company, Oakville, Ontario

Canadian Brewing Award Winners, 2008

Gold: Picaroons Best Bitter, Northampton Brewing Company, Fredericton, New Brunswick
Silver: ESB, Mill Street Brewery, Toronto, Ontario
Bronze: Swans ESB, Swans Buckerfields Brewery, Victoria, BC

India Pale Ale

The historical version of events as to how this beer got its name, supported by beer stalwarts like Michael Jackson, is that a brewer named George Hodgson of the Bow Brewery in London, England, added sufficient hops and gravity (alcohol content) to his pale ale in order for it to make the long trip to India in the late 1700s. Recently, there has been a lot of dialogue in the blogosphere disputing this story, but no one has been able to fully disprove it. Hodgson or not, India pale ale (IPA) is a beer known for its higher alcohol and hop content, and it has been enjoyed for centuries.

Today, traditional IPA is typically made with hard water and many hops, creating a crisp, dry, bitter beer, full of hop flavour and aroma. The colour is anywhere from a pale gold to deep copper. The alcohol content in these ales is often higher than the standard five-percent ABV, and as a result, fruity and caramel flavours may be noticed.

In Canada, our top-selling IPA doesn't come close to replicating the flavours and aromas that are expected for this style. Alexander Keith's India Pale Ale may very well have been a proper IPA back when Keith himself was heading up operations on Lower Water Street in Halifax, Nova Scotia, but today, his IPA is as generic as mass-marketed pale ale can be. Yes, Keith's IPA does have distinct hop flavour and aroma when compared to a mass-marketed North American lager, but that really doesn't say much. To all the Keith's fans out there, no disrespect, but try a true style-defining IPA—I'm sure you'll be surprised.

Canadian Brewing Award Winners, 2007
> ***Gold***:   Imperial Pale Ale, Garrison Brewing Company, Halifax, Nova Scotia
> ***Silver***:   Amnesiac Double IPA, Phillips Brewing Company, Victoria, BC
> ***Bronze***:   Hophead India Pale Ale, Tree Brewing, Kelowna, BC

Canadian Brewing Award Winners, 2008
> ***Gold***:   Imperial Pale Ale, Garrison Brewing Company, Halifax, Nova Scotia
> ***Silver***:   Hophead India Pale Ale, Tree Brewing, Kelowna, BC
> ***Bronze***:   Amnesiac Double IPA, Phillips Brewing Company, Victoria, BC

North American-style Amber/Red Ale
Very popular among the craft-brew set, this style of ale is set apart from other varieties by its use of North American hops, such as the Cascade. North American hops provide North American-style amber/red ales with a strong, bitter flavour and aroma. The colour of these ales can range from light copper to medium-red, bordering on medium-brown, which speaks to the malt and caramel flavours often present.

Canadian Brewing Award Winners, 2007

Gold: Blue Buck, Phillips Brewing Company, Victoria, BC

Silver: Race Rocks Amber, Lighthouse Brewing Company, Victoria, BC

Bronze: Irish Red Ale, Garrison Brewing Company, Halifax, Nova Scotia

Bronze: Tankhouse Ale, Mill Street Brewery, Toronto, Ontario

Canadian Brewing Award Winners, 2008

Gold: Yukon Red Amber Ale, Yukon Brewing Company, Whitehorse, Yukon

Silver: Cameron's Auburn Ale, Cameron's Brewing Company, Oakville, Ontario

Bronze: Fire Chief's Red Ale, Pump House Brewery Ltd., Moncton, New Brunswick

North American-style Blonde or Golden Ale

Often confused for lagers because of their colour and clarity, ranging from golden to straw, these ales are typically much dryer than their cold-fermenting counterparts. Despite the dryness, blonde ales aren't often hoppy, but they do possess a light maltiness, sometimes coupled with fruity undertones.

Canadian Brewing Award Winners, 2007

Gold: Piper's Pale Ale, Vancouver Island Brewing, Victoria, BC

Silver: Griffin Extra Pale Ale, McAuslan Brewing, Montréal, Québec

Bronze: Stock Ale, Mill Street Brewery, Toronto, Ontario

Canadian Brewing Award Winners, 2008

Gold: Stock Ale, Mill Street Brewery, Toronto, Ontario

Silver: Griffin Extra Pale Ale, McAuslan Brewery, Montréal, Québec

Porter

What is interesting about porter is that it can be made with both warm-fermenting ale yeast and cold-fermenting lager yeast. English-style porter is made with ale yeast and is heavily malted and lightly hopped. The bitterness experienced in an English-style porter is not necessarily from the hops, but instead from the use of black malt (malt roasted until black). English porters are dark brown to garnet and also contain fruity notes from residual esters.

Baltic porters, on the other hand, are lagers. This style of beer is widely consumed in the Baltic States, and it was here that Baltic brewers originally swapped ale yeast for lager yeast as the use of lager yeast rose in the 1800s. Baltic porters, like their ale counterparts, are dark, malty, strong beverages with fruity undertones and roasted malt notes. Little hop bitterness is present, while some bitterness from black malt may be perceived.

Canadian Brewing Award Winners, 2007

Gold: Black Oak Nutcracker Porter, Black Oak Brewing Company, Oakville, Ontario

Silver: London Style Porter, Propeller Brewing Company, Halifax, Nova Scotia

Bronze: Coffee Porter, Mill Street Brewery, Toronto, Ontario

Canadian Brewing Award Winners, 2008

Gold: Coffee Porter, Mill Street Brewery, Toronto, Ontario

Silver: John Sleeman Presents Fine Porter, Sleeman Brewing, Guelph, Ontario

Bronze: Man's Best Friend, Northampton Brewing Company, Fredericton, New Brunswick

Scotch Ale

Light amber to deep brown, these sometimes-smoky ales are malty with little-to-no hop flavour. The smoky profile in North American Scotch ales hearkens back to the beer's Scottish roots when brewers would sometimes dry their malt over burning piles of peat. With the Scotch-ale malty finish, notes of caramel may be evident. The high malt content often leaves this style on the low end of the ABV scale, typically around four percent.

Canadian Brewing Award Winners, 2007

Gold: McAuslan Scotch Ale, McAuslan Brewery, Montréal, Québec

Silver: Swans Scotch Ale, Swans Buckerfields Brewery, Victoria, BC

Canadian Brewing Award Winners, 2008

Gold: Scotch Ale, Pump House Brewery Ltd., Moncton, New Brunswick

Silver: Scotch Ale, Mill Street Brewery, Toronto, Ontario

Stout

Stout, like its name, is a full-bodied ale, and as its colour (rich brown to almost black) implies, it is a hearty take. That is not to say that all stouts are the same. Dry stouts use roasted unmalted barley to cut the malt and fruit flavours otherwise present. Imperial stouts are high-alcohol-content, extra-hopped ales, while other sweet stouts are less hopped and contain additions, such as oatmeal, that give the already full-bodied stout even more heft. Regardless the stout, most varieties contain roasted coffee and chocolate notes, as many stouts incorporate specialty malts in their brews, or a combination of unmalted and malted, kilned grains.

Canadian Brewing Award Winners, 2007

> **Gold**: Swans Oatmeal Stout, Swans Buckerfields Brewery, Victoria, BC
>
> **Silver**: Espresso Stout, Yukon Brewing Company, Whitehorse, Yukon
>
> **Bronze**: Keepers Stout, Lighthouse Brewing Company, Victoria, BC

Canadian Brewing Award Winners, 2008

> **Gold**: St-Ambroise Oatmeal Stout, McAuslan Brewery, Montréal, Québec
>
> **Silver**: Hockley Stout Traditional Irish Ale, Hockley Valley Brewing, Orangeville, Ontario
>
> **Bronze**: Cobblestone Stout, Mill Street Brewery, Toronto, Ontario

Strong or Belgian-style Ale

Even though these are sometimes considered specialty beers on account of the addition of coloured candy sugar, they still belong to the ale family. Typically between 6-percent and 11-percent ABV, these beers are malty and sweet. Belgian ales range in colour from very pale amber to deep burgundy. They also have little hop taste and are sometimes spiced with other herbs.

Canadian Brewing Award Winners, 2007

> **Gold**: Swans Legacy Ale, Swans Buckerfields Brewery, Victoria, BC
>
> **Silver**: St-Ambroise Vintage Ale, McAuslan Brewing, Montréal, Québec
>
> **Bronze**: Surly Blonde, Phillips Brewing Company, Victoria, BC

Canadian Brewing Award Winners, 2008

> **Gold**: La Fin du Monde, Unibroue, Chambly, Québec
>
> **Silver**: La Maudite, Unibroue, Chambly, Québec
>
> **Bronze**: Surly Blonde, Phillips Brewing Company, Victoria, BC

Wheat Beer—Belgian-style White, or "Wit"

Great for a summer day, this style of wheat beer is pale yellow to gold in colour, with a light, tart, sometimes-fruity finish. Whites are soft, quenching and light-bodied—a result of the unmalted wheat used along with the malted barley. Typical of wheat beer, whites are sometimes bottle conditioned (yeast left, or added, to the bottle to continue the fermentation process, creating natural carbon dioxide, higher alcohol content and sediment at the bottom of the bottle). Bottle conditioning can create a slightly bitter yeast taste; as a result, this style displays varying degrees of clarity. Belgian-style whites are mildly hopped and may contain notes of orange and coriander.

Canadian Brewing Award Winners, 2007
- **Gold**: Blanche de Chambly, Unibroue, Chambly, Québec
- **Silver**: Belgian-Style Wit, Mill Street Brewery, Toronto, Ontario

Canadian Brewing Award Winners, 2008
- **Gold**: Tessier's Witbier, Swans Buckerfields Brewery, Victoria, BC
- **Silver**: Belgian Wit, Granville Island Brewing, Vancouver, BC
- **Bronze**: Blanche de Chambly, Unibroue, Chambly, Québec

Wheat Beer—German-style Hefeweizen

About half the makeup of a Hefeweizen is malted wheat, and when this is coupled with higher levels of carbonation, the result is an extremely thirst-quenching ale. Hefeweizen hop rates are very low, and the flavours that dominate the palate are clove, nutmeg, vanilla and banana. Almost always bottle conditioned, Hefeweizen can be cloudy but possesses a slightly bitter yeast taste and fuller mouth-feel. Brewers often encourage drinkers to reintroduce the yeast sediment to their beer by swirling the bottle.

Canadian Brewing Award Winners, 2007

Gold: Muskoka Hefeweissbier, Lakes of Muskoka Cottage Brewery, Bracebridge, Ontario

Silver: True North Wunder Weisse, Magnotta Brewery, Vaughan, Ontario

Canadian Brewing Award Winners, 2008

Gold: Hefeweizen, Tree Brewing, Kelowna, BC

Silver: Denison's Weissbier, Denison's Brewing Company, Toronto, Ontario

Bronze: Whistler Weissbier, Whistler Brewing Company, Vancouver, BC

Wheat Beer—North American-style

Pale yellow to gold, even light amber in colour, this North American style is wide ranging, as both warm- and cold-fermenting yeast varieties can be used. Thirst-quenching, these soft ales and lagers are lightly hopped and slightly tart. Many craft brewers recommend serving this beer with lemon or orange on the rim of your glass.

Canadian Brewing Award Winners, 2007

Gold: Grasshopper, Big Rock Brewery, Calgary, Alberta

Silver: Sungod Wheat Ale, R&B Brewing Company, Vancouver, BC

Bronze: High Country Kolsch, Mt. Begbie Brewing Company, Revelstoke, BC

Canadian Brewing Award Winners, 2008

Gold: Sungod Wheat Ale, R&B Brewing Company, Vancouver, BC

Silver: Velvet Fog, Wild Rose Brewery, Calgary, Alberta

Lager

Bock—Traditional German-style

Originally, Bock was the beer that Bavarian monks drank while they fasted. The high-profile malt base gives Bock lagers a sweet, dense finish. The hop flavour and aroma is light to medium, while chocolate notes may be present. A Bock colour profile can range from light amber to deep brown. Typically, a Bock has a slightly higher alcohol content than a standard lager, reaching upward to seven-percent ABV. The Bock family has three other members: Doppelbock, a stronger version of this lager; Helles, lighter coloured and less dense; and Eisbock (Ice Bock), a lager brewed then frozen in order to extract ice-water crystals—the result of which is a brew with a higher alcohol content. You may be thinking this last process sounds familiar. That's because in North America, Labatt calls this "ice brewing." To this day, Labatt insists they invented ice brewing as a wholly new process when really it is a centuries-old German tradition.

Canadian Brewing Award Winners, 2007
> ***Gold***: Copper Bock, Canoe Brewpub, Victoria, BC

Canadian Brewing Award Winners, 2008
> ***Gold***: Helles Bock, Mill Street Brewery, Toronto, Ontario
>
> ***Silver***: Nickel Brook Ice Bock, Better Bitters Brewing Company, Burlington, Ontario

Light (Calorie-reduced) Lager

While this style of lager is technically classified as beer, the amount of adjuncts used, the incredibly low levels of hop and malt present and the amount of carbonation added leave this lager bland, pale, thin and gassy—more like soda-water than beer. That being said, if we're in the middle of nowhere and it's all we've got, I'd take one, please.

Canadian Brewing Award Winners, 2007

Gold: Jack Rabbit, Big Rock Brewery, Calgary, Alberta
Silver: Moosehead Light, Moosehead Breweries Ltd., Saint John, New Brunswick
Bronze: Steelback Light, Steelback Brewery, Hamilton, Ontario

Canadian Brewing Award Winners, 2008

Gold: Brewhouse Light, Great Western Brewing Company, Saskatoon, Saskatchewan
Silver: Coors Light, Molson, Montréal, Québec
Bronze: Moosehead Light, Moosehead Breweries Ltd., Saint John, New Brunswick

North American-style Amber Lager

As with most lagers, this style is meant to be clean and crisp with mild to mediate hop flavour and aroma. Amber lagers should possess more malt flavour than golden-coloured lagers, and amber-lager colouring—from copper to red—reflects the caramel overtones found in this type of beer.

Canadian Brewing Award Winners, 2007

Gold: Red Leaf Smooth Red Lager, Great Lakes Brewery, Toronto, Ontario
Silver: Harvest Lager, Bushwakker Brewing Company, Regina, Saskatchewan
Bronze: J.R. Brickman Amber, Brick Brewing Company, Waterloo, Ontario

Canadian Brewing Award Winners, 2008

Gold: Millennium Buzz Beer, Cool Beer Brewing Company, Toronto, Ontario
Silver: Dutch Amber, Amsterdam Brewing Company, Toronto, Ontario
Bronze: Red Leaf Smooth Red Lager, Great Lakes Brewery, Toronto, Ontario

North American-style Dark Lager

It is not rare to see a North American dark lager that is almost as black as Coca-Cola yet as clean and crisp-tasting as a standard golden lager. Although some special roasted malts are used, many North American dark lagers attain their complexion from adjuncts. As a result, these dark lagers are usually relatively thin despite their colour and are often heavily carbonated and somewhat sweet, carrying notes of caramel and sometimes chocolate. Malt flavours may be present, while hop flavours and aromas are seldom found.

Canadian Brewing Award Winners, 2007
Gold: Steelback Tiverton Dark Lager, Steelback Brewery, Hamilton, Ontario

Silver: Hermann's Dark Lager, Vancouver Island Brewery, Victoria, BC

Bronze: Black Jack Black Lager, Great Lakes Brewery, Toronto, Ontario

Canadian Brewing Award Winners, 2008
Gold: Cameron's Dark 266 Lager, Cameron's Brewing Company, Oakville, Ontario

Silver: Two Rivers Red, Fort Garry Brewing Company, Winnipeg, Manitoba

Bronze: Waterloo Dark, Brick Brewing Company, Waterloo, Ontario

North American-style Lager

This is your catch-all for North American lagers. Adjuncts such as corn and rice are found in this highly carbonated, straw- to golden-coloured lager. Although hops are used in this beer, hop flavour and aroma is usually negligible. Many people refer to this style as "lawnmower lager," as the only time it may be preferable to drink is just after you have finished mowing the lawn. There is no shortage of this class of lager at any pub or beer retailer.

Canadian Brewing Award Winners, 2007
   No winners declared

Canadian Brewing Award Winners, 2008
   Gold: Carling, Molson, Montréal, Québec
   Silver: Laker Lager, Brick Brewing Company,
              Waterloo, Ontario
   Bronze: Cool Beer, Cool Beer Brewing Company,
              Toronto, Ontario

North American-style Premium Lager

Straw- to golden-coloured, this lager, when made by a craft brewer, quite often uses no adjuncts in the overall finished product. If adjuncts are used, corn and other adjunct-like flavours are subtle—as is the hop flavour and aroma. Premium lagers have slightly more malt flavour than standard North American lagers, while both maintain a crisp, clean taste.

Canadian Brewing Award Winners, 2007
   Gold: Muskoka Lager, Lakes of Muskoka Cottage
              Brewery, Bracebridge, Ontario
   Silver: Golden Horseshoe Premium Lager, Great Lakes
              Brewery, Toronto, Ontario
   Bronze: Cameron's Lager, Cameron's Brewing Company,
              Oakville, Ontario

Canadian Brewing Award Winners, 2008
   Gold: Lighthouse Lager, Lighthouse Brewing Company,
              Victoria, BC
   Silver: Old Credit Pale Pilsner, Old Credit Brewing
              Company, Port Credit, Ontario
   Bronze: Great Western Premium, Great Western Brewing
              Company, Saskatoon, Saskatchewan

Pilsner

This variety of lager took the world by storm in 1842 when the first golden example was released. Up until then, beer had always been some shade of brown. Today, Pilsner is still the gold standard for a crisp lager with a light malt flavour balanced by aromatic hops. Many Pilsners have a dry, hoppy finish. No adjuncts, please! And, by the way, Labatt Blue is a North American lager posing as a Pilsner.

Canadian Brewing Award Winners, 2007

Gold: Walkerville Premium Blond, Walkerville Brewing Company, Windsor, Ontario

Silver: Kelowna Pilsner, Tree Brewing, Kelowna, BC

Bronze: Whistler Premium Export Lager, Whistler Brewing Company, Vancouver, BC

Canadian Brewing Award Winners, 2008

Gold: Pilsner, Mill Street Brewery, Toronto, Ontario

Silver: Rocky Mountain Genuine Lager, Fernie Brewing Company, Fernie, BC

Bronze: Traditional Pilsner, Creemore Springs Brewery, Creemore, Ontario

SPECIALTY BEER

What is a specialty brew? It is beer made with or processed using an ingredient or method that is outside convention. For starters, beer with additions of fruit, herbs, spices and the like can be considered a specialty brew, particularly if the special ingredient is a key component in the overall experience of the product. As well, additions or modifications to the brewing process, such as fermenting ale yeast at a warm temperature and maturing the resulting brew at cooler lager temperatures, can also create a specialty beer.

Basically, specialty beers are nothing short of fantastic. Their interesting additions and modes of preparation create unique flavour profiles, colours and aromas that are sometimes a welcome alternate from the everyday. The Belgians, the world's first specialty-beer makers, have been making unique and interesting brews such as Lambics and strong ales for centuries. There are also countless examples of specialty brews from other countries that have gone on to influence some of today's most inspired batches. Among these are German Rauchbier (smoke beer), which is created by drying malt over an open fire, thus infusing the malt with a smoke flavour; and California Common, an American lager matured in unconventional shallow vats at ale temperatures that create an amber, medium-bodied lager with ale-like malt complexity and hoppiness.

The Canadian Brewing Awards don't have a blanket category for specialty beer; instead, they have two categories focused on two different areas of specialty-beer production where Canadian brewers excel: Maple/Honey Ale and Lager, and Fruit and Vegetable Beer.

Maple/Honey Ale and Lager
Since the mid-to-late 1990s and around the time Sleeman launched its Honey Brown Lager in 1997, Canada has seemingly developed a taste for honey-brewed beer. The public perception of honey lagers is that they are a mark of distinction. The thirst for these lagers is especially prevalent in Ontario, where virtually every brewery attempting to gain a chunk of the competitive discount-retail segment has a honey-brewed lager in its portfolio. The problem, of course, is that just because you can dress up a discount lager, doesn't mean you should. Aside from very mild honey notes, these discount honey brands still have the hallmarks of mass-market North American–style lagers: thin body, adjunct flavour and high carbonation.

On the flip side, craft-brewed honey (or maple) beer uses the sugary addition together with malted grains, typically barley, in either a conventional or unconventional brewing process to create a beer that delivers a true premium lager or ale, supplemented by a maple or honey flavour that doesn't overpower the other aspects of the brew. It is important that the flavours are in proportion with one another, unless the goal of the beer is to subvert the style it is made in, thus making it an extreme beer (see page 131, A Modern Take: Extreme Brewing), in which the added maple or honey flavour will most likely dominate.

Canadian Brewing Award Winners, 2007

Gold: Niagara Honey Brown, Niagara Falls Brewing Company, Niagara Falls, Ontario

Silver: Steelback Tiverton Bear Honey Brown, Steelback Brewery, Hamilton, Ontario

Bronze: J.R. Brickman Honey Red, Brick Brewing Company, Waterloo, Ontario

Canadian Brewing Award Winners, 2008

Gold: Great Lakes Winter Ale, Great Lakes Brewing Company, Toronto, Ontario

Silver: Honey Brown, Niagara Falls Brewing Company, Niagara Falls, Ontario

Bronze: Old Credit Holiday Honey, Old Credit Brewing Company, Port Credit, Ontario

Fruit and Vegetable Beer

These lagers and ales are generally quite different in comparison to others in the lager and ale families. A vegetable beer, like a pumpkin ale, is medium-to-dark in complexion, full-bodied with notes of nutmeg and cinnamon and is drastically different from a fruit beer, such as a blueberry ale, whose complexion is much lighter with flavours nowhere near as heavy as those in its vegetable counterpart. Both fruit and vegetable beers can be made with whole fruits or vegetables or with extracts. Either way, the goal, of course, is to create a well-rounded beer with proportionate flavours for the given style.

Canadian Brewing Award Winners, 2007

Gold: Frambozen, Mill Street Brewery, Toronto, Ontario

Silver: Raspberry Wheat, Phillips Brewing Company, Victoria, BC

Bronze: Great Lakes Pumpkin Ale, Great Lakes Brewing Company, Toronto, Ontario

Canadian Brewing Award Winners, 2008

Gold: Longboat Chocolate Porter, Phillips Brewing Company, Victoria, BC

Silver: Pomegranate Wheat, Amsterdam Brewing Company, Toronto, Ontario

Bronze: Framboise, Amsterdam Brewing Company, Toronto, Ontario

THEY COME ABOUT LIKE THE SEASONS

Specialty brews aren't for everyone, and they aren't for every occasion, either. Beer, like clothing, can be tailored for the season. And so, just as you wouldn't wear shorts outside in the winter, a pint of Guinness wouldn't be your first choice on a muggy summer day. Drinking seasonal brew, whether curling up with a malty, high-gravity winter-warmer in front of the fireplace or having a light, quenching wheat ale in the summer months, is a very enjoyable pastime. Here is a list of some brew styles that you might enjoy in each season.

Spring

The damp, chilly, slushy end of winter and beginning of spring is the perfect time for the dark, often-strong Bock-style lager. Ranging from dark brown to almost golden, these lagers warm you up with their higher alcohol content but won't bog you down; the lager style keeps the brew mildly hoppy and lighter in finish than its strong-ale counterparts. As the spring months let on, move to lighter and lighter brews. The Maibock, or May Bock, are light, Bock-style lagers perfect for the end of spring.

Summer

Put the Corona down! There is more to summer than a beer that needs lime to hide the skunky taste of a brew packaged in clear bottles and shipped over long distances. Instead, enjoy a light, refreshing golden ale (sometimes labelled "summer ale") or a North American premium lager. You could also treat yourself to a citrusy, thirst-quenching wheat ale, or do as the Belgians do and enjoy a Saison—a bright, crisp ale originally made in Belgium for farm workers to quaff after a hard day working the land.

Authentic Saison-style brews are only made in the French region of Belgium, hence the French *saison*, which means "season."

Fall

What do the months October and March have in common other than 31 days? They were the original beginning and end of the brewing season. Before refrigeration was invented and yeast understood, brewers could only brew beer in the cooler months, as the warmer months led to higher rates of wild, airborne yeast that ruined their carefully executed craftsmanship. As such, beer was made throughout the winter and stored (often in caves) and consumed over the course of the summer. When October rolled around, it was time to polish off the last of the beer produced in March. In 1872, Josef Sedlmayr of Munich brewed his version of the red Vienna-style lager. Sedlmayr's brew was amber in colour, and as a result of aging, was slightly higher than usual in alcohol content. The beer, which he called Märzenbier, was produced in March, stored until September and then served at Oktoberfest where it became a German staple. As Michael Jackson explains it, that is why the words March (or Märzen) and October can sometimes be found on the same beer bottle.

In the fall, festivals abound celebrating the harvest with food and drink. It is German tradition to drink a Märzen or Oktoberfest beer at these festivals. Copper-to-red with a higher alcohol content than the five-percent ABV that is considered the norm in Canada, and with a malty makeup, these beers are perfect for crisp fall days. Brown ales, nut-brown ales and North American–style amber ales are also great fall accompaniments.

DID YOU  KNOW?

The first Oktoberfest was celebrated not for the harvest, but for the marriage in October 1810 of Bavarian Crown Prince Ludwig and Princess Therese. The king- and queen-to-be invited the citizens of Munich to celebrate the wedding on the fields in front of the city gates. These fields are now named Therese's Fields, or in German, Theresienwiese, which the locals simply refer to as Wiesen. The first of the royals' parties lasted five days, and subsequent parties were extended to the now-practiced 16 days, beginning in September and ending in October.

Winter

There is nothing like relaxing with your favourite Christmas sweater and a robust winter-warming beer. These are the beers that make you feel all cozy inside, and if you aren't careful, wobbly when you get up—so don't sit too close to the fireplace. Winter beers are typically amber to dark brown, very malty, high in alcohol content and are often spiced with a variety of spices, from nutmeg and cinnamon to juniper and anise. Barley wines are also popular winter drinks, as are Doppelbocks, stouts (especially oatmeal) and other dark beers.

GETTING DRUNK WITH THE ANCIENTS

Beer has come a long way to get where it is today: bottled, refrigerated and with multinational brands served around the globe that often outsell their local brethren. But just as anything else, beer evolved from humble roots and had to overcome hardship and persecution to get its current state.

Beer=Civilization?

As Homer Simpson states, "Beer is the cause of, and solution to, all of life's problems." The funny thing is, this bumbling four-fingered cartoon character is pretty much right. So right, in fact, that without beer, civilization might not have ever began.

As Peter Brown tells it in his book *Man Walks into a Pub*, beer and the process of fermentation were undoubtedly discovered by accident. Shortly after we were walking upright, we began to look for ways to alter our perception. It was during our time as hunter-gatherers that along with eating berries and twigs, we started collecting grain. From here, all it took to get us on the path to discovering beer was rain. As Brown says, we don't know when we took hold of the powers of fermentation, but if some of the collected, harvested and stored grains got wet, it was enough for the cycle of fermentation to begin. Once we tried the resulting mucky mixture, it wasn't long before we realized it was something we wanted to consume again.

So why did we settle down in one place? Was it to protect us from the elements and give us a home? Or was it because we wanted to make more beer? We can never really know the answer, but many anthropologists believe that beer played a significant part in humans wanting to settle. Which means, as Brown playfully surmises, drinking beer could hold the meaning of life.

Toronto Has the Key?

Although Toronto, a city established in 1834, probably doesn't have anything to do with the oldest known artifacts relating to beer, one of the city's residents, Dr. T. Cuyler Young Jr., certainly did in 1973. A research team led by Young— then-curator of the West Asian Department at the Royal Ontario Museum (ROM)—excavated the site of Godin Tepe, a Mesopotamian civilization in the Zagros Mountains of western Iran. It was here where jug fragments were found that closely resembled the Sumerian pottery used for the storage of barley beer. Beer pottery from the Mesopotamian era contains a grooved interior, and when the residue on the jug fragments was chemically tested, it proved the pottery was indeed used as a container for beer. The shards of residue date back to circa 3500–3100 BC, making them the oldest known beer-related artifacts in the world!

The ROM collected over 10,000 artifacts from Godin Tepe, and it is interesting to note that the site, specifically the same excavated room as mentioned, also held artifacts of the earliest known wine jars.

Bring Me One Jug and Two Straws!

Beer in Mesopotamia was less of a pure liquid as we experience it today; it was more of a mash. The "Hymn to Ninkasi," an ancient Sumerian poem to the goddess of beer (Ninkasi), includes one of the oldest recipes for beer. The poem speaks of a baked grain product that is soaked and stored in a jar, sometimes with aromatic spices. This was how beer was first developed, and why beer was more like a food than a drink.

With pulpy bread and grain husks still in the mixture, beer-chugging wasn't really an option. So to get around the problem of how to consume the best part of the beer—the liquid— Sumerians devised the straw, which did an acceptable job of eliminating the pesky husks and bready goop. A literal golden example, believed to be the first straw, was found in an excavation of the Mesopotamian city, Ur (modern-day Iraq). The golden straw was found in the tomb of a high priestess named Lady Pubai.

A Pint to Die For?

The Sumerians made beer a part of everyday life: they even had advertisements featuring curvaceous bare-breasted women and slogans like "Drink Elba—the beer with the heart of a Lion," but it was the Babylonians who really got serious about the drink.

New York's Metropolitan Museum holds an ancient tablet that lists the beers available to Babylonians. The list has beers on it that sound familiar today—dark beer, pale beer, red beer and beer with a head—and also includes two beers that induce some noggin-scratching: three-fold beer and beer without a head (while I can imagine this, I'm not aware of any beer today sans head).

We can deduce from this list that not only did Babylonians have more choice than Sumerians, but they also were never short-changed at the pub. When Hammurabi, the sixth Babylonian king, declared his code of laws to the Babylonian people, one law forbade a tavern-keeper from delivering a short measure. The punishment? Death, of course.

Come for the Pyramids, Stay for the Beer!

Death for a short pour seems a little extreme, but I like the ingenuity employed by Hammurabi. Wouldn't it be nice to live in a society where the consumer's needs are met and the value of beer is given the utmost importance? Well, if you could have your parents plan your birth to happen in Egypt and turn back the clock to, oh, 4000, maybe 5000 years ago, then you'd be in luck! The Egyptians were the true titans of the ancient beer-drinking world. The right to the fermented beverage was afforded to every citizen (including slaves), and everyone had a daily ration. And talk about fair prices: beer wasn't taxed until after Cleopatra took over rule of the land in 51 BC.

Beer was so important to the Egyptians that a mug of it, along with a loaf of bread, made up the markings of the hieroglyph for food. Beer was also used in the treatment of medical ailments, from boils to ulcers to scorpion stings.

For the Egyptians, beer was not just a right in waking life but in death as well. When a body was mummified and placed in its tomb, items for entertainment and sustenance were provided for the journey to the afterlife. Beer was one of the things left for the deceased's journey. There is nothing like a few cold ones when traversing to the other side!

"We Ran Out of Clean Drinking Horns."

"But we've got some boiled skulls over there. You might as well drink out of those."

That may not have been the dialogue, but it was certainly the case with the Vikings. As beer historian Alan D. Eames points out, when no drinking horns were available, the Vikings would sometimes boil the skulls of felled enemies and essentially drink from the bones. As if this ritual wasn't grotesque enough, Viking warriors also performed a blood-brother-type ceremony where one man bled himself into the beer skull of another warrior. It was said that only death could undo the bond that was created between the two men who drank the beer-blood concoction from the same skull of an enemy. If it was up to me, I'd settle for a high-five.

When not drinking out of skulls, Vikings drank out of exactly what stereotypical portrayals show—drinking horns. It has been said that because of the shape of the horn and

the resulting inability to set down a horn that was full of beer, the ale was often downed in one or two gulps. This is one explanation for why the Vikings were always so drunk— and maybe this is how and where chugging was invented? Another explanation for chugging down beer may be that people were measured by how much beer they could drink, much like the system that operates similarly in North American frat houses. It is unknown whether the Vikings held toga parties.

However, they did hold other types of parties. In fact, when storming a new village, the Vikings liked to go drinking with their foes. When the Vikings had heavily out-drunk the opposition, the warriors would leave and set fire to the pub with the passed-out villagers still inside.

 Vikings were a people of their word, so much so that any pledge made by a Viking while drunk was considered a legally binding statement.

Beer for the Ladies

You can thank beer for the terms "bride" and "bridal." Both words find their origins in the word "bru," which means "to brew."

In medieval Europe a "bride-ale," or bridal, was a party held at a wedding reception. The mother of the bride was in charge of brewing ale that was sold to wedding guests and passing travellers. The belief was that a weak beer would result in a weak marriage, so bridal beer was often strong. The price for the ale was marked up considerably, with all proceeds going to the bride's dowry. Bridals were so popular as fundraising events that the public was often notified by advertisement of the big party. Sometimes, however, too much was beer was brewed, and when this happened, the ale sales could continue for days, creating a very drunk public.

Groaning ale was another European beer tradition centred around the married woman. When a pregnancy was made public, the mother-in-law of the pregnant woman mixed up a batch of strong brew. The beer sat for the duration of the pregnancy until labour started (the time of groaning).

For added strength, the mother-to-be and the midwife then partook in the special strong ale. Once delivered, the baby was often bathed in the brew, as the beer was deemed cleaner than water. This tradition eventually made it all the way to the U.S., and according to Eames, lasted well into colonial times.

A BEER RENAISSANCE

The Law of the Land

To say that the Germans are serious about beer is like saying Canadians really like hockey. Both statements are supported by years and years of national profiling and stereotyping. But sometimes stereotypes exist because they are so spot-on. The fact of the matter is that Germans love their beer, and Canadians love their hockey.

In the case of German beer-loving, however, it could be said that one state in particular loves its beer more than any other state in Germany. The state in question is, of course, Bavaria, where in the spring of 1516 the co-rulers of Bavaria, Duke Wilhelm IV and Duke Ludwig X, introduced the Reinheitsgebot (the beer purity law). The original law stated that only three ingredients could be used in the production of beer: barley, water and hops. Yeast was not considered an ingredient of beer at the time, given that it hadn't yet been discovered; fermentation happened with wild, airborne yeast strains, and the process was still considered a magical transformation.

The Reinheitsgebot was designed to keep beer free of unwanted ingredients, such as wild mushrooms, and to ensure that brewers used barley as opposed to rye and wheat; the latter grains were kept for the better-suited purpose of bread production.

Yes, but what about all of the wheat beers the Germans love to quaff? Well, the Reinheitsgebot was the law in Bavaria only—the rest of Germany could do what it pleased. That is, until 1906 when the Reinheitsgebot became law throughout the entire country. The adoption of the law across Germany brought about a few changes: yeast was made an official

ingredient, and the use of other malts (including wheat) were allowed (alongside barley malt) in the production of ale.

The Reinheitsgebot was overturned in 1987, however, because it hindered free trade. But even though no longer considered law, many German brewers cite pride and tradition as reasons to still adhere to the Reinheitsgebot, and beer made within the law's strict regulations has become a symbol of prestige for brewers around the world. Even Canadian brewers, such as Steam Whistle Brewing, cite the beer purity law in reference to their choice of ingredients.

Ale Gets a Brother

Brewing was originally a task performed, for the most part, by women. This is because brewing, like baking, was executed as a daily event in the home. Furthermore, many of the deities that represented beer in the spiritual world were women. It wasn't until medieval European times that the men of Christian monasteries started taking the reins of the brewing industry.

Monks spent a lot of time making beer. Not only did they have to make beer for the other monks of the monastery, but they also had to provide beer for all of the people who helped run the monastery—and their families, too! This demand meant brewing time was precious. When the ale beer the monks made began to ferment, a rich froth formed on top of the brew. Some of this froth was then held back to help the next batch of beer ferment. However, this method of "top fermentation" was subject to the surrounding environment, and (as you now know) could be ruined very easily by wild yeasts that floated into the mix. And so, to recap, in an effort to protect the beer from these wild yeasts the monks began placing the beer in caves and packing the casks with ice to keep the beer cool. This resulted in a slower brewing process, but it also resulted in a new type of fermentation. The monks soon learned that, in colder temperatures, some of the yeast stayed at the bottom of the cask and fermented there instead of at the top. The monks eventually isolated the new type of yeast and continued to prepare the new "bottom fermenting" beer. The new beer was called "lager beer," named after its process of manufacture—"lagern"—which, as I mentioned previously, means "to store" in German.

Lager exploded onto the scene. It was a lighter-tasting alternative to the ales available. However, it was hard to produce en-masse given that it took longer to make in cooler temperatures. This relegated lager in its infancy to a seasonal beer that was only produced in the winter.

DID YOU KNOW?

Even though monks discovered lager, the beer the monastic tradition is most closely associated with today is the Trappist Ales of Belgium's Trappist monasteries. The hard-working monks who abide by the Trappist order live by the fruits of their labour alone, and that often means they need to sell their beer. Seven of the world's 14 Trappist monasteries brew beer for sale to the public. Six of them are located in Belgium: Achel, Orval, Chimay, Westmalle, Rochefort and Westvleteren, while the seventh, Koningshoeven, is located in the Netherlands. Trappist brew is readily sought after for its quality and high degree of craftsmanship. In order to protect the Trappist monasteries from opportunistic businesses looking to cash in on the Trappist brand, the International Trappist Association was created in 1985 to protect the interests of the Trappist identity. Authentic Trappist products are now marked with a special seal.

Brewers See the Light

Not at the end of the tunnel, but through their beer.

Lager beer, like ale, used roasted malts for brewing. These malts, when used in either the top-fermenting ales or bottom-fermenting lagers, made beer of the same complexion— dark brown. The world didn't witness a lager beer like the ones we are familiar with today—golden and delicious— until 1842, some 400-plus years after the discovery of lager.

The distinct characteristic of the lager created in 1842 was its colour. In the Bohemian town of Pilsen (Plzen), which is now in the Czech Republic, brewer Josef Groll decided that instead of roasting the barley to dry it, as was the custom, his brewery would air-dry the barley. The effect was a remarkable change in the colour of the malt. Not the traditional dark brown, the malt was a golden, straw-like colour, and the resulting lager was the same hue. This brew became known as Pilsner, named after the town where it was created.

The colour of this new lager was appealing, and more than that, was easily showcased as the use of clear glass was on the rise. Patrons visiting pubs that served Pilsner revelled in the delight of seeing the light through their beer. Pilsner became so popular, so quickly, that copycat Pilsners were made available all across Europe. In 1898, the brewery in Pilsen changed its name to Pilsner Urquell, a German phrase that means "from the original source, Plzen," in order to protect the brewery's legacy and cement its status as creator of the first true Pilsner. Today, any lager that is golden in colour owes itself to Josef Groll.

The Milk Man Loves his Beer

Louis Pasteur was a man of experimentation. It was Pasteur who, by unlocking the secret of micro-organisms, dispelled the myth that life was spontaneously generated. Before this discovery, it was widely accepted that certain life forms could arise spontaneously from inanimate matter. Pasteur's work with microscopic life forms in the mid-to-late 1800s explained the magical act of fermentation that many believed in for so long and essentially stripped beer from the almighty unknown and put its science in the hands of brewers. No longer was the spiritual other, Godisgood, doing the work. Instead, tiny,

Louis Pasteur

invisible-to-the-naked-eye organisms called yeast were exposed as the industrious little workers transforming barley mash into beer.

Beer of the National Revenge

Pasteur, a native of France, didn't want his findings on yeast to go to just any brewer. As Brown tells it in *Man Walks into a Pub*, Pasteur wanted some kind of national retribution after Germany humiliated France in the Franco-Prussian war (1870–71). Popular opinion of the day was that Germany developed the best beers in the world. So Pasteur decided that his contribution to the restoration of French pride was to beat the Germans at what they did best—beer-making. Thus, Pasteur took his studies on micro-organisms to England in 1871 and proved without a doubt that yeast did the job of fermenting, and that bad batches of beer were created because of competing yeast strains and other micro-organisms infecting the brewing yeast. In 1873, Pasteur further developed the production of scientifically superior brew— or as he called the beer resultant from his methods, *Bières de la Revanche Nationale* (Beers of the National Revenge)— by stressing the use of closed containers, germ-free air and carbon dioxide.

Pasteur's secrets more than likely ended up in the hands of Germans a few years later as his studies were published in 1876 under the title *Études sur la Bière* (Studies on Beer).

DID YOU  KNOW?

While pasteurization is widely referred to as a discovery first used in the production of milk, it is actually wine that holds this distinction. This fact shouldn't come as a surprise, given Pasteur's nationality. It was soon after his wine-pasteurization experiments that Pasteur began employing the process to beer and milk. Pasteur's work, *Études sur la Bière*, included findings on beer pasteurization, or "flash heating," which helped kill pathogens that caused beer to spoil. To employ flash heating, beer had to remain in contact with a source of heat between 71°C and 79°C for a period of 15 to 60 seconds.

A Gift From Denmark

Jacob Christian Jacobsen was a nice guy. Even better, Jacobsen was a nice guy with a lot of money, a brewery and a big crush on Louis Pasteur (not a sexual crush, but more of a man-crush—an unfounded loyalty based on respect and admiration).

When Jacobsen read *Études sur la Bière*, he immediately set out to create a modern laboratory to assist in the production of world-class beer at his Carlsberg brewery. By 1878, the laboratory was opened, and Jacobsen selected botanist Emil Hansen to head up the new digs. Hansen, familiar with Pasteur's work, decided it was his job to try to isolate a single strain of yeast, thus eliminating the competing strains that created bad batches of beer. It took him five years, but in 1883, Hansen cultured the world's first, pure single-strain of yeast, and because yeast reproduces by cell division, Hansen's single-strain was also a re-newable resource. This meant that every batch of Carlsberg beer was guaranteed to taste the same. In fact, the yeast Carlsberg uses today is a direct descendant of the yeast Hansen first isolated, which ended up being named *Saccharomyces carlsbergensis*.

Oh, and of that nice Jacobsen guy: when Hansen approached him with the proposal of creating a variety of pure yeast strains to sell to other brewers, Jacobsen insisted that the discovery at Carlsberg belonged to the world—pretty nice.

A Tasty, Cold Beer

The production of lager and the popularity of Pilsner led to the increased need for breweries to seek refrigeration. Before any form of artificial refrigeration existed, brewers harvested ice and used caves for their lagering needs. This system worked for decades when lager was only a seasonal, wintertime drink.

But as its popularity rose, ice harvesting became less efficient, especially because of problems with the pollution of water where the ice was being harvested.

A Contest Triggers a Revolution

Carl von Linde, a mechanical engineering professor at the Technical University of Munich and also another beer-minded man from Bavaria, began to research refrigeration because of a contest involving a cooling unit that was to be used for the crystallization of paraffin. Von Linde became enthralled with the idea of refrigeration, and he drafted his ideas in 1870 and 1871 for the *Bavarian Industry and Trade Journal*. He was subsequently courted by brewers looking for a year-round solution to their lager-production problems.

Von Linde's first refrigeration unit was used in 1874 in the Dreher Brewery, then the largest brewery in Austria, located in the city of Trieste (now part of Italy). The refrigeration unit wasn't stable and leaked methyl ether, the gas used as coolant. His second and third designs, which employed ammonia as opposed to methyl ether, became the standard for many years. From here, von Linde worked on many different ways to include refrigeration in the brewing process, including natural convection cooling (using coils) and carbon dioxide liquefaction cooling. All of this to meet the needs of his many suitors—including those at Heineken, Guinness and our old pal at Carlsberg, Jacob Christian Jacobsen.

IF YOU LIKE BEER SO MUCH THEN WHY DON'T YOU MAKE SOME?

Many Canadian men (and one woman) shaped their families—and as a result, Canada—around the brewing of beer. Without the Canadian brewers attached to these long-enduring names, we might not have grown up a beer nation. I'd just like to say one thing to these people: thank you!

John Molson

When it comes to the fraternity of North American brewers, none can claim the longevity and history of the Molson family. When 22-year-old John Molson, at the outset of his brewing empire, wrote in his notebook on July 28, 1786, in capital letters, "MY COMMENCEMENT ON THE GRAND STAGE OF THE WORLD," two months before even brewing his first beer, he had no idea his ambitions would be the start of North America's oldest and longest-surviving beer brand and brewery.

In January 1785, Molson took control of a brewery off the coast of the St. Lawrence River at St. Mary's Current outside Montréal. The story of the brewery's change in ownership from Thomas Lloyd to Molson is the stuff of legend and befits the kind of good fortune that greatness needs. In 1784, Lloyd, who was behind in payments to the brewmaster after only one year of operation, found the financial burden too much to bear and wanted to get rid of the brewery. This was two years after Molson's arrival to Canada as an 18-year-old, and despite the help he gave to Lloyd in operating the brewery, Molson was still too young to legally own it. So, he and Lloyd, with the help of the local sheriff, hatched a scheme that landed Molson the brewery. In turn, Lloyd moved out of the city to live on Molson-owned farmland near Lake Champlain.

The transaction was set into motion when Lloyd claimed insolvency in 1784, and as such, the brewery was put up for auction in December of that year. The public, however, was not made aware of the auction, and the sheriff noted that no bids were placed on the brewery. Shortly after the first auction, Molson turned 21 and the brewery was then put up for auction once more. Again, the public knew nothing of the auction, but this time Molson made the sole bid. And with that, the Molson brewing legacy began.

Molson died in 1836, the 50th anniversary of the founding of his company. In his will, he stipulated that an oil portrait of himself, finished in 1826, was to hang in the Molson boardroom for as long as the family owned the company. If ever the company was in "the hands of strangers," the portrait was to come down and be given to the descendants of his youngest son William's family.

After the February 2005 merger of Molson Inc. and the Adolph Coors Company, John Molson's company today is called the Molson Coors Brewing Company. When Molson crafted his will 173 years ago, he surely didn't anticipate anything like this merger, but he would be proud to know that the company still rests in his family's hands and his portrait graces the wall in the Molson fourth-floor conference room in Montréal at 1555 Notre Dame Street East.

Molson the Sailor-man

In building his empire, patriarch Molson did more than brew beer. In 1809, construction was completed on his first ship, the *Accommodation*, Canada's first steamship. Launched on November 1 of that year, the *Accommodation* was 26 metres long and driven by a six-horsepower engine. The vessel represented an accelerated way of travelling from Montréal to Québec City; it also opened new expedited trade opportunities. By 1813, the *Accommodation* was dismantled, and the *Swiftsure* took her place, with Molson's youngest son, William, as the 19-year-old captain. In 1814, the *Malsham* was added to the fleet, and in 1817, the Molson family's fourth steamship, the *Lady Sherbrooke,* was launched. The *Lady Sherbrooke* was a luxury steamship with a 63-horsepower engine that could make the trip to Québec City from Montréal in 23 hours—a far cry from the eight days the *Swiftsure* took to get there. The steamship fleet eventually grew to 22 vessels, which the family had interest in until 1855.

Molson the Banker-man

In 1818 John Molson, after some initial hesitancy, joined as a shareholder and director in the newly formed Montréal Bank. The Montréal Bank operated for six years as an independent outfit before receiving its charter from the British government in 1822, at which point it was named the Bank of Montréal. On June 9, 1826, after almost two years of inconsistent leadership and underperforming stock, Molson became the president of the Bank of Montréal. The bank eventually regained its credibility and stocks began to rise. Molson stayed on as president until 1830.

Twenty-four years after Molson left his presidency at the Bank of Montréal, his son William was granted formal charter for Molsons Bank, a bank he had been running since the year previous (1853). William served as president of the bank, and John Molson Jr. (John Sr.'s oldest son) as vice-president. In 1870, the family chose London, Ontario, as the site for the bank's first branch outside of its original operation in Québec. The Molsons grew their banking empire to 177 branches across Canada by 1925, at which point they merged with the Bank of Montréal to create the largest bank in Canada at that time.

Molson Highlights

With a family legacy that is over 200 years old, the story of the Molsons could fill many volumes—and it has—so instead, here are some highlights:

- In 1819 John Molson Sr. was one of three men to form a delegation to establish the Montréal General Hospital—Montréal's first public hospital. Later that year, Molson donated £1000 to the building fund of the Montréal General Hospital. When the hospital received its official charter in 1823, Molson and his three sons all sat on the board of directors.

- John Molson Sr. rebuilt his famous Mansion House Hotel in 1825 (which had burned down four years earlier in March 1821) and renamed it the Masonic Hall Hotel (later changed to the British American Hotel). Beside this new hotel, Molson commissioned the building of the Theatre Royal, Montréal's first permanent theatre and Canada's first permanent housing for performing arts.

- Canada's first railway, the Champlain and St. Lawrence Railroad, travelled southeast from La Prairie, Québec, on the St. Lawrence River, to St. John's, Québec, on the

Richelieu River in order to help ease travel to New York. Conceived of by Jason C. Pierce, the railway's principal financer was John Molson Sr., with a contribution of £36,000. The railway was incorporated in 1832 and officially opened in the summer of 1836. Molson died in January of that year and never saw the railway operate, but John Jr. was appointed as the railway's first president and William was on the board of directors.

- On July 6, 1852, fire broke out in the Molson Brewery in Montréal. In fact, fire ravaged a good part of the St. Mary's suburb of Montréal that night, and legend has it that 61-year-old Thomas Molson, middle son of John Sr., stormed into the inferno to save the family's important documents. Some stories say Thomas, with ledgers clutched in his arms, escaped by leaping from a window to firefighters below; others say he smashed through a second-storey window with the family strong box and that the box was lowered to safety while Thomas hurried out the window and was brought down on the shoulders of a firefighter. The brewery was adequately covered by insurance and was later rebuilt bigger and better, of course.

- In 1907, the brewery's yearly output exceeded one million gallons. And only two years later, in 1909, the brewery reached the output milestone of two million gallons in one year.

- February 15, 1945, saw Molson Brewery Limited (the company name adopted in 1911 when it became a private limited joint-stock company) become a publicly shared joint-stock company with 150,000 shares going for $20 each on the Montréal Stock Exchange. The move signalled the first time the brewery was open to ownership outside the family.

- In 1989, Molson Brewery entered into a partnership with conglomerate Elders IXL of Australia (Fosters), who took control of 40 percent of the company. The merger gave Molson control of the Carling brand, which Elders had purchased two years earlier in 1987. In 1999, Molson regained outright control of its operations with a $1-billion buyout of Elders, while still retaining the Carling brands.

Alexander Keith

The gregarious and giving nature of Alexander Keith has become romanticized in the modern-day notion of "Nova Scotia good times." Although there is truth to Keith's celebrated generosity, he was also a business stalwart who helped establish the city of Halifax.

Keith learned the brewing trade from an uncle in Sunderland, northern England, and in 1817, the 22-year-old came to Halifax and was immediately installed as brewmaster for Charles Boggs and his brewery. Three years later, Keith purchased the brewery from Boggs and renamed the venture the Nova Scotia Brewery. In 1822, Keith moved from the original brewery site to a larger facility on Lower Water Street, where he expanded the brewery again in 1836. (This is what visitors are treated to today when visiting the historical site.) A year after the second expansion, Keith was made a director of the Bank of Nova Scotia, as well as a director of the Halifax Fire Insurance Company. The latter appointment was the beginning of what was an active role in the utilities and insurance sector of Halifax, as Keith was involved in or helped found the Colonial Life Assurance Company, the Halifax Marine Insurance Association, the Halifax Gas, Light and Water Company and the Halifax Water Company.

Keith held the office of mayor of the City of Halifax three times; he was first elected in 1843, and again 10 years later for two successive years in 1853–54. Keith also acted as the leader of the freemasons in Halifax, becoming Grand Master of Nova Scotia in 1869.

In 1853, Keith's son Donald became a full partner in the brewery, which was renamed Alex. Keith and Son. The partnership lasted 20 years until the death of the elder Keith, at which point Donald assumed full control. Unfortunate for the company was Donald's business acumen, and the brewery steadily lost ground in the Halifax beer market. Donald did not have any heirs, so the company was split among his sisters after his death. The brewery remained in operation and within the family until 1928 when fellow Halifax citizens and the Keiths' rival, the Olands, purchased it.

Today, AB InBev (an amalgamation of Anheuser-Busch, Interbrew and the Brazilian-based AmBev) owns Alexander Keith's, as the Nova Scotia brewer was part of the Labatt acquisition of the Oland brand in 1971, and therefore part of the Interbrew purchase of Labatt in 1995.

John Kinder Labatt

John Kinder Labatt emigrated from Ireland to Upper Canada in 1833. He became a farmer in the London, Ontario, area, and, known for his barley, Labatt made many friends in the brewing game. In 1847, he joined Samuel Eccles as a partner in purchasing London's Simcoe Street Brewery, which was renamed Eccles & Labatt. Labatt apprenticed under the senior brewer Eccles for close to 10 years, at which point Eccles, in 1855, sold his half of the brewery to Labatt, giving him full control. The brewery became known as John Labatt's Brewery, but John only saw 11 years of his brewery operations. He died

in 1866. His son, John Jr., maintained the family business, renaming it Labatt & Company. John Jr. got his start in brewing with a family friend, George Smith, four years after John Sr. took full control of the Eccles & Labatt operation. Smith owned a brewery in West Virginia, and it was there that John Jr. apprenticed and learned the fine art of brewing— he even created his own recipe for India pale ale, which became popular as a Labatt product when he stepped up as owner of his father's brewery.

When John Jr. died in 1915, his two sons, John S. and Hugh, were named heads of the company. Made a limited company in 1911, Labatt was a corporation at the time of John Jr's death. It is said that until John Jr.'s death, all but four shares of John Labatt Limited were in his control. After he died, each of his nine children (two sons, seven daughters) was given equal share in the company. The private corporation became a publicly traded company in 1945 (the same year as rival Molson) with 900,000 shares issued and 2000 different shareholders.

John S. died in 1952 and Hugh in 1956, upon which time the management of the company was passed on to W.H.R. Jarvis, the first non-family president of Labatt. Jarvis suffered a heart attack two years later and, as a result, the first-ever elected non-family president became John H. (Jake) Moore, who was first brought into the company fold in 1953 while Hugh was in charge.

The company left the family trust in 1964 in a complicated buyout that originally saw the American brewer Schlitz take control of the company until the American government claimed antitrust; a conglomeration of three Canadian companies then purchased the brewer. Labatt became a foreign-owned company in 1995 when the Belgium-based company Interbrew purchased the then-148-year-old brewery. Today Labatt is owned by AB InBev.

The Sleemans

The Sleeman family legacy lay dormant for over 50 years between 1933 and 1988, until the Sleeman brand that Canadian beer drinkers are familiar with today was reintroduced to Canada in the late 1980s.

Upon his arrival in Canada from England in 1834, John Sleeman made sure he was a part of the North American brewing industry. Between 1836 and 1856, he founded two breweries, leased a third and worked for two others. His first foray into the Canadian brewing world was with the Stamford Spring Brewery, which he opened in 1836 in the Upper Canada community of St. David's, just outside St. Catharines, Ontario. After nine years in St. David's, Sleeman sold the Stamford Spring Brewery and left for New York, where he worked as a brewmaster at a brewery in Lockport. In 1849 the patriarch of the Sleeman brewing family returned to Canada and leased and ran James Hodgert's Brewery in Guelph only to leave two years later and open his own brewery in that city: the Silver Creek Brewery. Five years into the operations of Silver Creek, Sleeman was forced into bankruptcy and moved to manage yet another brewery in Guelph.

By 1859, Sleeman had compiled enough capital to regain his Silver Creek Brewery. The brewery, founded in 1851, became the base for the Sleeman family legacy, as it was passed on to his son George in 1867.

George Sleeman took his father's drive and dedication and coupled it with a business savvy that made Sleeman's Silver Creek Brewery the most profitable brewing company in Ontario by 1890. George's business directives included the introduction of steam power in the 1860s, lowering prices below those of the competition and the implementation of a vertical integration production and distribution model that saw Sleeman products available in 15 distribution centres across Ontario and Québec.

His success with the Silver Creek Brewery also helped him become the first mayor of Guelph in 1880, a position he held for two years and reclaimed twice: 1892 and 1905. George's ambition and love for the community of Guelph led him to privately finance an electric streetcar line for the city in 1894. After laying eight kilometres of track with the hope of neighbouring communities joining in the venture, Sleeman went insolvent and lost the streetcar operation, his house and the brewery to the bank in 1902. In 1906, his last year in office as mayor, the bank sold him back the brewery.

During his four-year stretch without Silver Creek, the Sleemans opened the Springbank Brewery. Upon reclaiming owner-ship of the flagship Silver Creek Brewery, George merged the two operations under the title George Sleeman and Sons Limited, which was overseen by George Sr. and his three sons, George A., Fred and Henry.

George Sr. died in 1926, the same year the Silver Creek Brewery was sold to local Guelph rival, Holliday Breweries. Henry continued to operate the smaller Springbank Brewery until 1933 when his brother, George A., was caught smuggling beer across the U.S. border into Detroit. The family was given an ultimatum by the Canadian government: pay back the beer taxes and sell the brewery, or lose possession of the business outright. The family paid the taxes and sold the brewery, effectively ending the 82-year-old family business.

In 1988, thanks to John W. Sleeman, the family brewing legacy was officially revived as the 90-year-old cream ale recipe from John W.'s great-great-grandfather was once again produced and poured—this time in a brand new $10-million state-of-the-art facility.

John W. learned of his family legacy in 1984, from his aunt, and set out to revive the Sleeman tradition. With multiple investors, including the U.S. brewing company Stroh's, John W. secured the funding necessary to rebuild a Sleeman brewery. Incorporated as Sleeman Breweries Limited in 1996, the already-competitive brewery continued to grow into what became Canada's third-largest brewer with a series of regional acquisitions, including Okanagan Spring and Shaftebury in BC and Alberta, the Upper Canada Brewing Company in Ontario, Unibroue and Seigneuriale in Québec and Maritime Beer in Atlantic Canada.

Today, Sleeman Breweries Limited is no longer Canadian-owned. In October 2006, Sapporo Breweries Limited of Japan (whose North American brewing and distribution is handled by Sleeman) purchased controlling interest of the reincarnated Canadian brewer. John W., the founder of the contemporary Sleeman brewery, remains involved with the company as chair and CEO of Sleeman operations.

DID YOU  KNOW?

John W. learned of the family brewing legacy when his aunt gave him some of the original glass beer bottles from the then-defunct company, as well as a leather-bound book containing the original Sleeman recipes. It is said that the cream ale recipe Sleeman uses today is the same one created many decades earlier, and that the trademark clear glass bottles are replicas of the bottles originally used by the family.

Thomas Carling

Thomas Carling arrived in Upper Canada as 21-year-old in 1818 and started a farm off the Thames River, outside what is now London, Ontario. He earned quite a reputation among the locals as a home-brewer and even had requests for his brew from the nearby military barracks. In 1843, after moving his family into London, Carling opened a brewery in the city, strategically located across from the military barracks, where his primary customers lived. In 1849, Carling's two sons, William and John, purchased the brewery from their father and renamed it W. and J. Carling's City Brewery. John, while holding the position of brewery president, became involved with politics and eventually ended up as Canada's minister of agriculture. Sir John (knighted in 1893 by Queen Victoria) died in 1911, and upon his death, his son Thomas, who had been an official partner in the family business since 1875, took up the Carling brewery helm. He was the last Carling to head the family business before E.P. Taylor purchased it in 1930.

In 1989, Carling O'Keefe (the name given to the company in 1973 as a result of the Canadian Breweries–Rothman merger) merged with Molson. Today, Carling is brewed in Canada as a discount lager by Molson Coors.

Eugene O'Keefe

While the family name of O'Keefe remained one of the most recognized brands in the Canadian brewing industry well into the 1980s, the company's patriarch, Eugene O'Keefe, founder of the Canadian institution, was the first and last of the O'Keefe clan to ever run the iconic brewery.

O'Keefe, not a brewer by trade, was a savvy businessman who, before brewing, was involved in the hotel industry, grocery trade and banking business. So, his decision to enter brewing was purely for business reasons. It was in Patrick Cosgrave and George Macaulay Hawke that O'Keefe found a brewmaster and a business partner when he needed know-how and capital in order to purchase the Victoria Brewery in the community of York, Ontario, in 1862.

Cosgrave left the effort in 1863 in order to start up another brewing franchise in the city, the West Toronto Brewery, which was run by the Cosgrave family until E.P. Taylor purchased it in 1934.

After Cosgrave's departure, O'Keefe and Hawke operated the Victoria Brewery as O'Keefe and Company until 1882, when O'Keefe's partnership with Hawke ended. In this 19-year period, the duo saw production increase dramatically, and as a result, the brewery was twice expanded, first in 1872 and again in 1882.

Hawke's replacement was his son Widmer, who partnered with O'Keefe in 1882. With the younger Hawke, O'Keefe expanded the brewery again in 1889. This expansion saw O'Keefe install the first mechanically refrigerated storage area in a brewery in Canada. The refrigerated storage area was needed because O'Keefe was one of the first brewers in Canada to produce lager on a large scale, a beer that the company introduced in 1879.

The 1889 expansion was not enough—it was twice replaced by larger, more modern and more efficient plants between 1891 and 1911. The last full-scale replacement marked the end of O'Keefe's time at the helm of the company. Devastated by the unexpected death of his only son Eugene Bailey in 1911, O'Keefe sold a 60-percent interest in the company to his partner Widmer, and the other 40 percent to Sir Henry Mill

Pellatt—the man who built Toronto's Casa Loma. O'Keefe Sr. died two years later, in 1913.

In 1934, the then-named O'Keefe Brewing Company Limited was purchased by E.P. Taylor, the same year he purchased Cosgrave's West Toronto Brewery.

E.P. Taylor merged with Rothman's of Pall Mall Canada Limited in 1968, and in 1973 the entire brewing operation that was known as Canadian Breweries was renamed Carling O'Keefe, as Rothman's wanted to inspire beer drinkers with the great family heritages the company contained.

Today the O'Keefe brand is owned by Molson Coors, who distributes both Old Vienna Lager (O.V.) and O'Keefe's Ale as discount brews.

The Olands

The Oland family brewing legacy is one that could have very well left us long ago. But thanks to the resilience of the Olands, and some healthy family rivalries, the Oland name has become synonymous with beer in the Maritimes.

It all started in the year of Confederation, 1867. For years, Susannah Oland had brewed her brown October ale to great fanfare, and it was while living in a rented house in Dartmouth, Nova Scotia, that a plan was hatched to sell her beer to the people of Dartmouth and Halifax. Susannah's husband, John, and family friend Captain Francis de Winton partnered with local businessmen George Harvey and Thomas Mowbray in August 1867 to open what was called the Army and Navy Brewery, in the Dartmouth region of Turtle Grove that fronted onto Halifax Harbour. John, out of work and relatively new to Canada from England, had no money to contribute to the business endeavour, but was named partner and manager. Susannah, whose recipes and expertise were used for brewing, had no legal stake in the brewery.

The company was well received but ran into uncertainty in 1870 with the death of John in a tragic horse-riding accident. Without any shares in a company founded on her family recipe, Susannah was helpless to take financial control of the brewery, and local businessman George Fraser purchased controlling interest in 1874. Fraser kept Susannah's sons John and Conrad on as brewers while he modernized the Turtle Grove facilities. Three years later, in 1877, Susannah bought back the family brewery with money inherited from relatives in England; the Turtle Grove facilities were renamed S. Oland, Sons and Co. (The "S" being Susannah's first official link to the company.)

Between 1878 and 1893 (also during which time the business was restructured as a joint-stock company) tragedy thrice stuck the iconic brewing family: fire twice gutted the Turtle Grove premises, and in 1886, matriarch Susannah died. However, the biggest wallop was yet to come.

On December 6, 1917, at 9:04:35 PM, Halifax and Dartmouth were rocked by what was then the largest human-made explosion in history. The explosion, known today as the Halifax Explosion, occurred after the empty Norwegian relief ship *Imo* collided with the munitions-loaded French vessel the *Mont-Blanc* in the narrows of Halifax Harbour—against which the S. Oland, Sons and Co. brewery stood. The *Mont-Blanc* had close to 2600 tonnes of munitions onboard and was headed for the war effort in France, while the *Imo* was set to sail to New York to pick up relief supplies bound for war-torn Belgium.

The result was catastrophic. Over 1950 people died, thousands more were injured and 12,000 buildings were damaged while

1630 were destroyed. The Turtle Grove brewery was demolished; seven workers perished, including Susannah's son, Conrad, the head brewmaster at the time.

But just as the family had in the past, the Olands—John and his youngest brother George—persevered through the tragedy.

Just one year after the explosion, with insurance money from the Turtle Grove brewery, George and his oldest son George B. negotiated the purchase of the Red Ball Brewery in Saint John, New Brunswick. The Olands were back in the business of brewing, and John acted as brewmaster. Colonel Sidney Oland, another son of George, returned to Halifax in 1925 after his tour of duty in World War I and a stint in Hollywood. Upon his return, Sidney took it upon himself to resurrect the family business in Halifax, which he did on the site of the former S. Oland, Sons and Co. brewery.

Three years later, in 1928, Sidney directed the purchase of the Alexander Keith brewery, which had been in the Keith family since 1820 and had always been the Olands' main competition. In the same year, the Olands also purchased the James Ready Brewery of New Brunswick (originally founded in 1867), which became the Moosehead Brewery. By the end of 1928, the Olands owned four breweries and had a firm grip on the Maritime beer market.

But boys will be boys, and the two brothers in charge of running the breweries, George B. and Sidney, had a deep rivalry. After the death of the George Sr. in 1933, the family fractured between the Nova Scotia Olands (Sidney) and the New Brunswick Olands (George B.).

The Nova Scotia Olands operated their company under the umbrella Oland and Son Limited, with three breweries in the company trust: Red Ball, Keith's and the rebuilt Oland

brewery. The New Brunswick Olands ran their brewery under the name Moosehead Breweries Limited. The name Moosehead was used when the James Ready Brewery was bought and it was discovered that the brewery had licensed a name for a beer that had never been produced: Moosehead. Needing a name that was distinct from the other Oland brands on the market, it was decided that the already-registered Moosehead moniker was perfect. In 1931, Moosehead Pale Ale was launched.

Today, the families are still split apart, though the Nova Scotia Olands are no longer owners of their namesake. In 1971 Labatt purchased the Oland and Son Limited holdings for just under a reported $11 million. Labatt gained the entire portfolio of Oland family beers—most notably Oland Export and Alexander Keith's—which are now part of the AB InBev family.

Moosehead, on the other hand, likes to call itself Canada's oldest independent brewery. While Moosehead Breweries Limited was technically formed in 1947, the family legacy dates back to 1867, and so does the original James Ready Brewery, purchased by the Olands in 1928. This author will let them have the distinction of Canada's oldest independent brewery, though, given that the family seems so tough! On April 1, 2008, Andrew Oland, no fool himself, took over as president of Moosehead to become the sixth generation to lead the Oland family brewing business.

DID YOU KNOW?

James Ready beer is still available. When the Olands purchased the James Ready facilities in 1928, they didn't have a beer to call their own upon moving into the brewery so they continued making James Ready's beer for the New Brunswick public. The beer remained available after the Oland family launches of both Moosehead and Alpine Lager, but, alas, James Ready was last sold in the Maritimes in 1990. Today, James Ready exists only in Ontario in the discount lager segment. The James Ready line carries three beers: James Ready 5.5, James Ready Honey and James Ready Light—all produced by the "James Ready Brewing Company"—which is actually the Niagara Falls Brewing Company, the Ontario-based brewery for Moosehead Breweries Limited.

The James Ready 5.5 recipe is the same recipe the Olands inherited when they purchased the Ready brewery in 1928.

E.P. Taylor

Edward Plunkett Taylor, better known as E.P. Taylor, or Eddie Taylor, is the man most often cited for creating the shape of the beer industry in Canada—and he wasn't even a brewer! Taylor was a businessman whose family happened to run a brewery, and it was with his "Grand Design" that he constructed a Canadian brewing empire that vastly altered the way Canada's brewing industry operated. Through his program of mergers and acquisitions, Taylor pioneered what is now common in the beer trade: the business of doing more business by buying out other competing businesses.

It all started in 1928 when the 27-year-old Taylor was on the board of directors for his family's company, the Brading Brewery of Ottawa. During this time, Taylor studied the landscape of the Canadian brewing industry, in particular the brewing industry in Ontario. His studies showed that the profits of the 37 breweries operating in Ontario were only half of what their combined assets were worth. He surmised that this poor performance was likely the result of too many breweries offering too many brands; the best way for the industry to be an efficient one was to have fewer brands and fewer, larger breweries.

The stock-market crash of 1930 came on the heels of the end of Prohibition in Ontario in 1927. Brewers who had survived Prohibition were heavily hit when the market crashed, and this was the perfect time for Taylor to begin his plan of acquisitions and mergers. Of course, money was hard to come by, and Taylor had to enlist the help of a partner. With investment of his own and from his partner Clark Jennison,

as well as Brading Brewery stock, Taylor took control of a total
of 10 breweries in 1930, the most important of which was the
Carling brewery. Taylor and Jennison incorporated the new
10-brewery company as the Brewing Corporation of Canada
Limited.

Between 1930 and 1935, nine more Ontario breweries were
added to the Brewing Corporation's fold, with Toronto's O'Keefe
brewery the prize catch in this round of acquisitions. Taylor
also became the sole head of the Brewing Corporation of
Canada when Jennison died in 1931.

Taylor's original plan had involved shutting down many of
the breweries he had taken over and consolidating his business to include only the largest, most efficient breweries
with the best regional locations. But with the Depression in
full swing, the Brewing Corporation of Canada couldn't
sustain any loss of potential market or volume output as the
company was staying solvent only by the thinnest of threads.
The Brewing Corporation of Canada didn't post a profit
until the end of 1935.

Over the course of the next 20 years, the Brewing Corporation
of Canada, renamed in 1937 to Canadian Breweries Limited,
had taken control of, shut down or consolidated 27 Canadian
breweries from coast to coast and also had interest in breweries in the U.S. and the UK.

To illustrate the influence Taylor's buyouts had on the beer
industry in Canada, you only have to look at Ontario, as the
37 brewing companies that existed in the province in 1928
shrunk to five by 1958. Furthermore, by the mid-1950s
Canadian Breweries Limited had reduced the overall brand
count that its breweries produced from a high of 27 to a low
of no more than eight. Taylor's practice of mergers and buyouts created an eat-or-be-eaten mentality in the industry,

and as such, big companies like Molson and Labatt started their own merger procedures in order to keep pace. The big guys in the industry haven't looked back since.

In 1968, Taylor himself opted for takeover, when Rothman's of Pall Mall Canada Limited purchased Canadian Breweries Limited for $28.8 million.

 In 1860, as many as 159 breweries were operating in Canada.

SOME SHORT STORIES FOR A SHORT HISTORY

The First Canadian Brews

Just like the first societies of the rest of the world, the Native peoples of this country used what they had when it came to making clothing and tools, collecting food and making drink. So, it is no wonder that when the first settlers from France and England arrived on our shores and made their acquaintance with the Natives, the foreigners were offered a beer-type drink made of spruce.

The first brew in Canada made of grain, thus beer, is credited to French herbalist Louis Hébert. Hébert emigrated from Paris to Québec in 1617. He is better known as Canada's first permanent settler, as he was the first to establish agriculture and capably live off the land. Part of his agricultural production was wheat and barley, and it is with these products, grown on his own land, that Hébert and his wife brewed their own beer.

The First Canadian Brewery

The land here wasn't the easiest to settle on—"cold" and "tree-filled" were the pluses when settlers wrote home to tell family of their new lives. So it is no surprise that it took these settlers a while to get a brewery up and going. In fact, it wasn't until 30 years after Hébert's landing in Québec that the Jesuit Brothers of Sillery constructed a brewery and one of them, Brother Ambroise, began brewing. The Sillery brewery was for the Jesuit Brothers' own use and wasn't open to the public. In 1650, three years after Brother Ambroise made his first brew, Louis Prud'homme started the first public brewery: a wooden structure located outside the city walls of Québec City.

The country's next brewing venture didn't come for another 20 years. In 1670, after three years of preparation, which included cultivating his own hops, Jean Talon, the first intendant appointed to New France in charge of justice and finance, opened *La Brasserie du Roi* (The King's Brewery). The brewery kept the 2000-plus residents of Québec City in drink, plus supported the French government with exports of beer to the West Indies. During Talon's two terms as intendant (1665–68; 1670–72) the population of New France grew from 3200 to 7600 people, and along with the brewery he founded sawmills, a shipyard, a shoe factory and a tannery. The King's Brewery, however, deemed less important to New France as wine and spirits became more affordable to import, ceased production shortly after Talon's departure as intendant and was totally decommissioned by 1674.

Canada's First Kidnapping for Ransom!

Kidnapping, ransom notes, manhunts and aliases. It is the stuff of Hollywood, but for the Labatts in 1934, it was all too true. John Sackville Labatt has the distinction of being Canada's first kidnapping-for-ransom victim. The crime was talked about across the globe and grabbed front-page billing on many newspapers, including the *New York Times*. On the morning of Tuesday, August 14, 1934, on his way to a company meeting, Labatt was snatched by a group of three men who, to the police and public, were known collectively as the singular "Three-fingered Abe."

The Labatt kidnapping was a three-day ordeal that took place across 400 kilometres: southwestern Ontario to Cottage Country in the Muskokas and finally to a peaceful ending in Toronto.

Upon following Labatt's car from his summer home outside Sarnia, the three kidnappers trailing him, Michael McCardell, Russell Knowles and Albert Pegram, confronted Labatt when they sped in front of his car and forced him to stop. The kidnappers then forcibly detained Labatt, though he sustained no injuries. McCardell and Pegram (with Labatt in their car) made for their hideout in Bracebridge, near the cottage resorts of Muskoka. Knowles stayed behind in order to drive Labatt's car to London, where it was deposited in the parking lot of St. Joseph's Hospital with a ransom note underneath the driver's seat. On the front of the note, mastermind McCardell had forced Labatt to write a brief letter pleading for his brother Hugh to deal with the kidnappers; the back of the note held the gang's demand of $150,000 (over $2 million today) and details surrounding the next communication, which was to come at the Royal York Hotel where the hand-off for the ransom was to be negotiated. The letter, signed "Three-fingered Abe," demanded silence in order to guarantee the safe return of Labatt. Knowles, referring to himself as Three-fingered Abe, placed a call to Hugh notifying him of the kidnapping and Labatt's car's whereabouts.

Pegram dropped off McCardell and Labatt at the hideout and was then supposed to drive back to Toronto where he was to meet up with Knowles in order for the pair to see through the ransom delivery with Hugh. Pegram never showed, however, and after waiting until Wednesday, Knowles left to inform McCardell.

McCardell and Knowles, defeated and worried about the possibility of Pegram snitching, drove to Toronto Thursday night and dropped Labatt off at 12:30 AM Friday morning on the corner of St. Clair and Vaughan, leaving him unharmed and with $1—enough to get a cab to the Royal York Hotel where his brother had been instructed to wait. Unbelievably, Labatt walked into the Royal York unnoticed by the throngs of police and media and went to the front desk and asked to be taken to his brother's room.

In 1935 McCardell was sentenced to 12 years in prison after pleading guilty to kidnapping Labatt, while Knowles was sentenced to 15 years. Pegram was never caught.

DID YOU KNOW?

John Sackville Labatt's kidnapping in 1934 wasn't the first time someone had attempted to abduct him; nor was it the first time the eventual kidnappers had conceived of kidnapping a member of Canada's liquor industry.

In 1933, Labatt and his family, out on the waters of the St. Clair River (bordered by Michigan on the south and Ontario on the north), were involved in a chase with a rum-running boat and would-be captors. Although reports of how the incident happened are conflicting, what remains the same throughout the various accounts is that the criminal element was frightened off.

In 1931, the mastermind of the eventual 1934 Labatt kidnapping, Michael McCardell, along with an assembled gang, planned to kidnap Samuel Bronfman, head of the Seagram Company. The gang followed Bronfman for two days in Montréal and expected to carry out the kidnapping on the third day. But after throwing a premature victory party for themselves, a drunk member of the gang was arrested for posing as a police officer. The kidnapping plan was dropped for fear that the arrested member might talk.

The First American Takeover of a Major Brewery—Sort of

In February 1964, the Joseph Schlitz Brewing Company of Milwaukee, Wisconsin, grabbed controlling power of John Labatt Limited, as over a period of six months the American brewer had negotiated with the 75 family and public shareholders to buy a 39-percent interest in the company. The purchase marked the end of the Labatt family exercising control over the 117-year-old company. It would not, however, mark the end of the company being Canadian-controlled.

What looked like a done deal, as was lamented by newspapers across Canada, was not so. Before the ink could dry on the cheques written by Schlitz for the Labatt shareholders, the United States Department of Justice declared the deal an antitrust violation that gave Schlitz an unfair advantage in the U.S. marketplace.

How? Well, Labatt owned majority interest in the General Brewing Corporation, a large California brewing outfit whose major competitor was another Californian brewer, the Burgermeister Brewing Company, which was owned by Schlitz. Despite the American brewer's best efforts to convince the U.S. government that it had no plans of duelling in California and instead wanted to seek expansion in Canada, the Joseph Schlitz Brewing Company lost the antitrust suit and was forced to sell off its stake in John Labatt Limited. As Allen Winn Sneath points out in his book *Brewed in Canada*, not only was Schlitz forced to sell off its holdings in Labatt, but it also had to sell Burgermeister and was not permitted to purchase any other breweries in the United States until 1976, which was 10 years after the court ruling. And Schlitz had to pay the legal tab—talk about rough!

Three separate Canadian companies purchased the 39-percent interest Schlitz had briefly owned: Jonlab Investments, Brazilian Light and Power, and Investors Mutual of Canada. The president of Labatt at the time of the takeover was John H. (Jake) Moore, who, along with other Labatt executives, held Jonlab shares; Moore retained his position.

DID YOU KNOW?

The actual first-ever American takeover of a Canadian brewery was in 1897. After declaring bankruptcy, the Kootenay Brewing, Malting and Distilling Company of BC was put up for auction. A winning bid of $25,000 was tendered, and a few months later the Yuengling Brewing Company of Pennsylvania took over operations of the brewery.

Carling Black Label—via E.P. Taylor— Takes Over Europe

These days, it's not a rare instance for a number-one-selling beer in any given country to come from a foreign brewer, especially given that two beer companies, AB InBev and SAB Miller, own the majority of the beer world. But 20 years ago when the world's beer industry was much less a conglomeration of multinational companies, this was not the norm. Defying that norm, however, the bestselling lager in Britain for the last 20 years has been a foreigner. And not just any foreigner, but a Canadian!

It all started in 1953 when the British brewery Hope and Anchor signed a partnership with Canadian Breweries that saw Hope and Anchor brew Carling Black Label in England in exchange for the Canadian Breweries' brewing and distribution of Hope and Anchor's Jubilee Stout in Canada. This partnership opened the door to the UK for E.P. Taylor and became the sequel of his aggressive takeovers in the Canadian beer industry—if it were a movie, this foray by Taylor might be called *E.P. Taylor Takeover 2: Electric Boogaloo*.

Carling Black Label, introduced in 1927—the year Prohibition ended in Ontario—was a popular beer in Canada and the U.S., but this did not mean much in the UK where the preference bent toward dark, bitter ales. The beer industry in the UK operates differently than it does in Canada, and the main difference is the "tied-house" system: a system whereby pubs are tied to breweries and feature their products. When Carling Black Label was introduced to the UK in 1953, it was immediately included in the 200 pubs that were tied to Hope and Anchor. With an immediate distribution chain, the hard work of getting the beer exposed to the drinking public was already done.

But 200 pubs wasn't enough exposure for Taylor, who was voracious in his pursuit of profit. In the next seven years, through his already-practiced formula of mergers and acquisitions, Taylor took the UK brewing industry by storm, forming a holding called United Breweries and amassing a tied-house count of almost 3000 pubs. Much like Molson and Labatt had in Canada, the UK beer industry reacted with their own mergers and acquisitions in order to keep pace with Taylor's methods. Unfortunately, in both instances, many regional brews were sacrificed.

In 1967, after merging with the British brewer Bass, Taylor succeeded in dong something he couldn't accomplish in Canada: his company became the biggest fish in the pond (in Canada he was always running behind Molson or Labatt in the market-share race). As a result, Carling Black Label— a Canadian lager—was the first lager distributed nationally in the UK. This didn't mean the English all of a sudden liked lager, but it was there.

Taylor retired from beer life in the UK in 1972, but Carling Black Label continued to soldier on, as it and other lagers like Heineken and Carlsberg proceeded to cram their way into the consciousness of the non-lager-drinking Brits. From 1993 to 2001 Carling sponsored the Premier Football League (soccer) and currently sponsors the League Cup, known as the Carling Cup. Carling Black Label (now just called Carling) is owned by Molson Coors.

The First Canadian Beer Can

The first Canadian beer can on the scene was marketed by Ben Ginter and his Prince George, BC, Tartan Brewing company in 1966, 33 years after the first beer can, the flat top, hit the market in the U.S. The beer in question, Tartan

Pilsner, was marketed under the name Pilcan Beer. This drew the ire of Carling Breweries as they already had a Pilsner released in BC that went by the nickname "Pil." Carling sued Ginter and, initially, the judge ruled in favour of Ginter and Tartan Brewing:

> *On a comparison of the labels and cartons used by the defendant and the plaintiff respectively, it cannot be said that a purchaser of Pilsener [sic] beer would be deceived or confused or misled into believing that the defendant's beer was the plaintiff's beer. There is just no appreciable similarity in the labels or cartons that would cause or be likely to cause confusion. The plaintiff does not sell its Pilsener [sic] beer in cans. The defendant does not sell its Pilsener [sic] beer in bottles. The cartons are as unalike as two beer cartons can be, both in shape and colouring.*

However, on an appeal, it was brought to the attention of the court that Ginter's Tartan Brewing had previously marketed beer under the names "High Life," "Paap's" and "Budd"—obvious infringements on the trademarks of American brewers Miller (High Life), Pabst and Budweiser (or Bud). As Sneath notes in *Brewed in Canada*, Tartan Brewing was ordered to stop using the Pilcan name and to give all of the Pilcan-related packaging to Carling.

 In an interesting twist, the Miller Brewing Company sued Carling O'Keefe in 1978 for trademark infringement because Carling O'Keefe had issued a brand of light beer called Highlite (obviously similar to Miller's High Life brand). The court ruled in favour of Carling O'Keefe, but nonetheless, Carling still changed the beer name to Trilight.

The Canadian Beer Bottle Story

Since 1933, our neighbours to the south have built their home-consumption beer industry largely around the can. Canadians, on the other hand, have predominantly enjoyed their home-consumed beer out of bottles.

The Growler

Before there were any retail outlets that sold beer, we brought our beer home from the pub, tavern or inn—in bottles. The first bottle Canadian beer drinkers started carting home was the growler. The growler held about two litres of brew and was the beer conveyance of choice in the late 1800s and early 1900s for those leaving the pub who wanted a little something for when they got home. Lore has it that the first growlers were nothing but galvanized buckets, and that the name "growler"

came from the sound of the beer sloshing around in the pail as it was carried home. Growlers, now made of glass or plastic with resealable caps, still exist and are used by brewpubs and home brewers for bottling purposes.

The Stubby

In 1962, the Canadian brewing industry adopted the first Industry Standard Bottle, affectionately known as the "stubby." Before the stubby, each brewery used a variety of its own bottles—anything from the 650 to 750 millilitre bombers and quarts to the first incarnation of tall, long-neck bottles. The brewing industry brought in the stubby as a cost-saving measure, because each brewery had a small fortune of individual bottle floats on hand at all times that required valuable warehouse space. With the introduction of the stubby, 24-million-dozen bottles were ordered nationwide, and by 1963, beer drinkers in every province and territory were sharing the same experience. The stubby was utterly efficient: its squat size and almost no neck gave it a low centre of gravity that allowed production lines to run quickly and smoothly. The stubby also took up less space in the warehouse and was easy to package. With all brewers using the same bottle, returned stubbies didn't have to be sorted, and as such, bottle-return rates improved dramatically. The stubby was built for a projected lifespan of 20 sale-return-wash-label-refill-sale cycles (known as the closed-loop container-return system) but often lasted 30, and sometimes 40, cycles. To production managers, the stubby was perfect. To sales and marketing executives, it was an eyesore. The stubby lacked sex appeal. It handcuffed executives and creative types who previously set their beer apart from the herd by placing it in an attractive package. The stubby's product uniformity made this impossible; consumers had to choose their suds based on what was *inside* the brown glass—bad news for a lot of brewers!

The Heidelberg Affair

The first attempt at subverting the stubby was in 1970 when Carling (then called Canadian Breweries) launched a brand named Heidelberg Ale. The beer was introduced at an interesting crossroads of national taste preferences, with the West largely preferring lager-style beer and Ontario and eastward still favouring ale—but that changed. What made Heidelberg a 10-percent market draw right out of the gate was its packaging. Both ale and lager drinkers were enamoured with Heidelberg's keg-shaped bottle: it was wide and barrel-shaped like a keg, with a long neck on top—with a screw cap to boot—which allowed it to stand out among the sea of stubbies. Labatt and Molson immediately took offence to the Heidelberg bottle that went against the stubby, and they claimed that Canadian Breweries was in breach of the Industry Standard Bottle agreement made in 1962. Canadian Breweries refuted that there was no such agreement and held out as long as they could. A year later, in 1971, after mounting pressure from the breweries and environmental agencies worried about a return to an individual glass-bottle system, Canadian Breweries released Heidelberg Ale in a stubby—a $1.3-million hit to the company that had already invested big bucks into Heidelberg's initial launch. With Heidelberg selling by only what was *in* the bottle, sales eroded and regional taste preferences triumphed. It would be another 13 years before anyone else decided to rattle the cage with a non-conforming bottle.

The Long-neck

The summer of 1983 in Canada was one of American import beers and tall bottles. Since the Heidelberg drama of 1970–71, the laws governing Industry Standard Bottle use were relaxed in order to allow every company two bottles in their portfolio that were non-conforming. By May 1983, Labatt had released John Labatt Classic in a green long-neck bottle, and Amstel (a Heineken subsidiary brewing out of Hamilton) had released its Amstel Lager in a long-neck. A few weeks later, Carling O'Keefe released Miller High Life in a long-neck bottle. Being an American import as well as a beer sold in a long-neck bottle made High Life a clear choice for many Canadians that year, and the brew swallowed up a market share of close to eight percent.

The Twist-off
In 1984, Labatt countered with the twist-off long-neck bottle, and in 1985 Molson launched Coors and Coors Light in long-necks. The stubby was essentially given up for dead in 1984, and thus we saw the start of the 10-year period of private-mould bottles.

Private-mould Bottles
It took the Canadian brewing industry 22 years to return to the inefficient, individual, non-returnable, non-refillable bottle system it once sought to rid itself of in the early 1960s. Brewers were once again required to have hundreds of thousands of dollars' worth of private-mould float bottles on hand at all times. The environmental agencies, so worried about the Heidelberg bottle 14 years previous, could only sit by and watch.

A consolation for the tree huggers, however, was the private-mould-era application of the Applied Ceramic Label (ACL). The proponents of the label proclaimed an environmental victory, as using an ACL meant fewer paper labels—good thing!

The Industry Standard Bottle
In 1994, coming off the heels of the recession, Canadian brewers once again established an Industry Standard Bottle, and the brown, long-neck twist-off bottle we know today was born. With the standard bottle, the closed-loop container-return system was implemented once more, and the Birkenstock, granola-eating crowd rejoiced. The group

that wasn't happy was the new microbrew sector. With the oldest microbreweries 10 years old at the time, it was a financial burden for the small operations to ditch their private-mould bottles and install new bottling hardware. It wasn't any easier if a brewer decided to stick with a non-conforming bottle, as sorting fees were introduced for those who didn't adopt the new standard bottle. Many new microbreweries simply couldn't afford the switch and closed, while others barely made it. All of this meant that for a brief time, those who supported the reuse initiative introduced by the Industry Standard Bottle but also wanted to support locally brewed small-market firms had a tough choice to make.

Today, the Industry Standard Bottle is a worldwide leader in efficiency and environmental responsibility. Seventy-three percent of the pre-packaged beer consumed in Canada is out of the Industry Standard Bottle, and 97 percent of those bottles (over three billion per year) are returned.

A TEMPERAMENTAL TIME

What to do About All This Tomfoolery?

Temperance wasn't a new thing when Prohibition hit Canada in the late 1800s. Without fail, the first public drunk created the first public call for alcohol moderation, and as the drunks multiplied, so, too, did the people opposing such intoxication. The temperance movement itself is defined by its dependence on the liquor industry. Like any group that is morally opposed to an action, that action has to exist. The problem for Canada in the 1800s was that the act of getting drunk was popular— so popular, in fact, that in the 1870s, Montréal boasted one bar for every 70 citizens, and in boomtowns near the Klondike gold rush, the pubs never closed. As a result, serious opposition to drunkenness was growing steadily. Temperance unions began to form in earnest long before the 1800s but really began to collect steam in the second half of the 19th century.

The first major coup for the temperance societies across the country trying to stem the tide of drunkenness was the establishment in 1864 of the Dunkin Act—not the Drunkin Act— named after Christopher Dunkin. The Act gave each municipality and county in Ontario and Québec the power to decide

whether it wanted to be dry. Under the Act, a population could declare itself dry if a vote was held and the majority of citizens consented to prohibiting the sale of alcohol. The Act remained viable after the incorporation of Nova Scotia, New Brunswick, Québec and Ontario into the Dominion of Canada in 1867, and by 1877, Ontario had 11 counties and 32 municipalities that were dry.

DID YOU  KNOW?

In 1874 the Liberal government enacted the "secret ballot law," which gave voters the opportunity to cast their votes secretly. The law also forced the closure of all bars on the day of a federal election. The government hoped these two actions would reduce the amount of barroom bribery and intimidation rampant within the old open-ballot system.

Great Scott!

In 1878, the Dominion of Canada passed the Canada Temperance Act, or, as many people knew it, the Scott Act—named after its main proponent Sir Richard William Scott. The Scott Act essentially broadened the scope of the Dunkin Act and was applicable in all the provinces under the control of the Dominion of Canada. The Temperance Act was first enforced in Fredericton, New Brunswick, and it was immediately opposed. The 11-year-old Dominion hadn't yet figured out which concerns were federal and which were provincial. The provinces argued that the Act itself was a violation of the provincial jurisdiction over liquor licences and property and civil rights, while the federal government countered that the Act was about peace, order and good government for the entire country—essentially public safety and moral well-being. The Act was upheld as constitutional by the Supreme Court in 1880 but was a continuous source of frustration for decades and was challenged numerous times. The Canada Temperance Act was law until 1984, when it was finally repealed.

Laurier: Good Guy, Still a Politician

In 1893, Liberal party leader Sir Wilfrid Laurier promised Canadians a national vote on Prohibition if his party was elected to office. The appointment to office by the people of Canada didn't happen for Laurier and the Liberals until 1896, and it took two more years for Laurier to honour his word. In 1898 a plebiscite was established, but only the men of the country were invited to vote. The turnout was 543,073 voters, which represented a scant 44 percent of the electorate. The result of the vote was 278,380 for Prohibition and 264,693 against Prohibition, a difference of 13,687 votes. As far as the public was concerned, and especially the temperance leagues, this was a huge victory. Prohibition values had won, and Canada was about to become a dry country. But Laurier, as a politician, changed his mind, and after citing the slim margin of victory for the prohibitionists versus the equally small percentage of the total electorate that was in favour of Prohibition (23 percent), Laurier decided that the Liberal government would not honour the vote. What was, for a brief instant, music to temperate ears became mere political rhetoric. Many accused Laurier of being sympathetic to the liberal-supporting Québecois who largely voted against Prohibition. Regardless, Laurier would not recant his position, and the ruling stood, never coming back to a nation-wide vote again.

That Unfortunate Time Called Prohibition

Prohibition wasn't necessarily a state of being for all of Canada. Yes, Canadians suffered Prohibition, but it was not like what was enacted in the U.S. Unlike our neighbours who lived under the statewide Volstead Act—the zero-tolerance policy on production, distribution, importation and sale of alcohol— Canada was relatively lax.

After the 1898 national plebiscite, the issue of Prohibition remained in the hands of each individual province as outlined in the terms of the Canada Temperance Act. Prince Edward Island was the first to enact Prohibition, doing so in 1901, and by 1917, the rest of the Canadian provinces had followed suit—minus Québec, which never really saw full-scale Prohibition, as the province continually allowed the production of wine and beer, only ever imposing bans on hard liquor. The years between 1901 and 1917 saw the temperance leagues work across Canada, creating a patchwork quilt of dry and wet communities.

The one time that the federal government forced nationwide Prohibition on Canadians was during World War I, as a measure to help the war effort, not necessarily to curb consumption. The War Measures Act of 1917—created three years after the beginning of the war and after every province had already decided for itself to enact some level of Prohibition— put the production of liquor at a standstill, as any grain that could be used to manufacture food was not to be used to make potable liquor products. That being said, industrial alcohol products were still made for the war effort, and Canadian brewers could produce temperance brews (beer rated at 2.5-percent ABV, which was heavy-hitting compared to the non-intoxicating 0.5-percent malt beverages the Americans were treated to a few years later).

The War Measures Act was only legislated to stay in effect for one year after the signing of world peace, and as a result, the bill was repealed in 1919, one year after the end of World War I. Enforcement of Prohibition was again transferred back to the individual provinces.

Through the Loophole

Prohibition enacted on a provincial level left many loopholes for those who still wished to imbibe. Thirsty people in provinces ruled by Prohibition got creative with their visits to the doctor. In most provinces, alcohol wasn't banned for medicinal or spiritual purposes; that meant the church could have wine at service, and doctors could still prescribe alcoholic remedies. It has been well documented that some doctors gave brazen amounts of alcoholic prescriptions, with figures ranging from hundreds to thousands per month. It

was also well satirized that lineups at the pharmacy quadrupled around the holidays during Prohibition years.

In Ontario it wasn't illegal to make beer; furthermore, it wasn't illegal to sell beer, either. Brewers just couldn't sell it within the province. This created the phenomenon of "mail order" beer. An Ontarian wanting to purchase beer wrote to a merchant in Québec with their intent to purchase beer and with their payment enclosed. The merchant then placed the order with a brewery in Ontario and mailed the receipt back to the Ontarian who purchased the beer. The Ontario customer went to the Ontario brewery with the receipt showing the out-of-province purchase and legally picked up the paid-for beer.

A few temperance brew names: Walkerville Brewing Company: Continental Lager and Scotch Boy Ale; Kuntz Park Brewery: Lagerine; John Labatt: Cremo; Rose and Laflamme Ltd.: Wanna Beer.

Windsor to Cuba Four Times a Day!

When the Volstead Act in the U.S. was made reality in 1920, brewers and distillers in Canada ventured into some murky waters, both figuratively and literally. The Detroit River, the link between Windsor, Ontario, and Detroit, Michigan, which at parts is less than one kilometre wide, was a key crossing point that is estimated to have seen 85 percent of the liquor that made it into the U.S. during Prohibition.

The river was home to bootlegging speedboats, while the Ambassador Bridge and the Detroit-Windsor Tunnel (also known as the Detroit-Windsor Funnel) were also used as

bootlegging conveyances. At bootlegging's peak, an estimated 500,000 bottles of booze per month were smuggled into Detroit. Boats full of liquor leaving Canada only had to claim *not* to be going to the U.S., which allowed them passage. Popular "destinations" cited by boat operators were Cuba, Mexico and South America. In fact, the Mexico Export Company, a one-boat bootlegging operation running docks out of Windsor, was recorded by Canadian customs to have made four trips from Windsor to Cuba in one day!

Bootleggers also used other points of entry to smuggle Canadian booze into the U.S. Small Canadian planes packed with alcohol often made stops in Long Island to unload, while many rumrunners, the most famous of which was William McCoy—whose booty was so good it was dubbed "the real McCoy"—set sail for the U.S. eastern seaboard from Saint-Pierre and Miquelon, French islands just off the coast of Newfoundland.

Beer was nowhere near as popular with bootleggers as whiskey was. Beer kegs were cumbersome to smuggle, and bottles, while smaller, didn't yield as much bang for your buck. Hardly any alcohol went into the system of speakeasies and blind pigs without being cut, and other than adding water, beer wasn't the easiest to work with. Whiskey, on the other hand, was potent, easily portable and easier to cut—perfect for a bootlegger's needs. But that didn't mean Canadian brewers were absent from the smuggling scene. Labatt had their own runner named Edmund Burke, and most famously, the Sleeman Family had to give up the family business as a result of bootlegging interests.

The illegal parade to the U.S. by Canada's liquor industry was put to a halt with the abolition of the Volstead Act on December 5, 1933.

The Cash Grab

As people found more and more loopholes in the Prohibition system, the patchwork quilt of dry communities the temperance leagues had worked so hard to construct began to unravel across Canada. The first two provinces to become "wet" were BC and Québec in 1920, followed by the Yukon in 1921, Manitoba in 1923, Alberta and Saskatchewan a year later in 1924, Newfoundland in 1925, Ontario and New Brunswick in 1927, Nova Scotia in 1930 and Prince Edward Island in 1948. Each province was required to put the decision to a vote, and upon repeal, each province, instead of going back to a private-retail model, opted to keep control of the liquor industry. Each province created control boards or commissions (often the same ones that operate today) to manage the liquor industry and generate income for the province. The business sector was probably not the happiest, but the citizens who wanted to drink didn't care.

DID YOU  KNOW?

The end of provincial Prohibition didn't mean that a community couldn't declare itself dry. Many communities stayed dry and became havens for supporters of the temperance movement. The Toronto neighbourhood of the Junction enacted Prohibition in 1904 and remained dry until 1997. Three communities in Nova Scotia—Cambridge, Maitland and Tidnish—didn't become "wet" until 2005, while the Manitoba towns of Hanover and Stanley stayed dry until 2006.

THE FIRST CRAFT BREWERS

BC Leads the Way

The eastern provinces of Canada were the first to be settled, and as a result, were the first to develop many of Canada's industries, including brewing. BC, therefore, was pretty late getting into the brewing game when compared to its counterparts in the Maritimes, Québec and Ontario. But despite BC's late blooming, the province holds an important role in the revitalization of the Canadian brewing industry following the age of Big Label domination that essentially wiped out independent brewing in Canada.

In June 1982, Canada's first brewpub and microbrewery opened in BC in the Horseshoe Bay area of Vancouver; the pub was called Troller's, and the microbrewery was the Horseshoe Bay Brewery. The founders, John Mitchell and Frank Appleton, convinced the BC government to grant them a brewing licence and to create legislation that allowed brewpubs. Under the new law, however, the brewery was not allowed to be attached to the pub, and the seating was limited to 65 patrons. The Horseshoe Bay Brewery and Troller's stayed in business for only a short while, because after a year of operations, the investors and the founders came to an impasse over ideological differences. Mitchell and Appleton left, and the brewery closed shortly afterward.

All was not lost, and as a direct result, Mitchell, with Appleton and Paul Hadfield, launched Spinnakers Brewpub in Victoria in 1984. While Mitchell and Appleton are no longer part of Spinnakers, it has become one of the premier brewpubs in all of North America, with Hadfield and his team offering not only quality hand-crafted ales, but a bed-and-breakfast-style resort with 10 guest houses, all just steps away from the award-winning brewpub and Spinnakers' wine-tasting bistro.

 The terms "microbrewery" and "craft brewery" are often used interchangeably, but the smart beer consumer knows the word "microbrewery" refers to a brewery's output volume, which often varies by region but as a general rule doesn't reach more than 20,000 hectolitres per year. A craft brewery, on the other hand, can exceed 20,000 hectolitres, but like many microbreweries, is typically a brewery that deals in small batches using all-natural ingredients with no additives or preservatives.

1984: Not Just a Good Book

The seminal year in Canada's beer renaissance was 1984. In this year, Canada's brewing scene leapt from the brewpub to the craft brewery, as three major craft breweries opened their doors.

Granville Island Brewery, Vancouver, BC

Granville Island Brewery was the first of Canada's craft breweries. Opened by Mitchell Taylor in Vancouver, BC, in June 1984, his path to brewing history is similar to that of other Canadian craft-brew pioneers. Taylor was inspired to brew beer after a trip to Bavaria. Much like John Mitchell of Horseshoe Bay Brewery fame, whose inspiration came from touring the last remaining original pub breweries in England, Taylor's eureka moment came from tasting independent Bavarian beers that were abundant in flavour compared to what was available in Canada.

The results of Taylor's efforts to broaden Canada's beer landscape were twofold. Granville Island Brewery became the first craft brewery to bottle its own beer for sale to licensed establishments—something the Horseshoe Bay Brewery could not do—and it is the first Canadian brewery to create an authentic German-style lager that cited compliance with the German purity law, the Reinheitsgebot.

Today, the original Granville Island Brewery is little more than a boutique brewery used to brew small batches of select seasonal brews. The company is owned by Canadian vintner giant Andrés Wines, and most of its brewing is done in Kelowna, BC.

Big Rock Brewery, Calgary, Alberta

In Alberta, Ed McNally founded the Big Rock Brewery of Calgary in September 1984. McNally's brewery made a name for itself by using all-natural ingredients that complied with the Reinheitsgebot. The brewery also made a strong contribution to the Albertan economy, choosing to use select two-row barley from Alberta farmers—as the former head of the Western Barley Growers Association, McNally knew a thing or two about the quality of Alberta's barley crop. The Big Rock Brewery's first brew was Traditional Ale, which is still one of the brewery's bestsellers. The brewery also added a porter and a bitter (neither of which are still in production) to its portfolio, giving the proud Canadian brewery a distinctly international flavour. In 1988, Big Rock made a big splash at the Winter Olympics in Calgary, as its international classics struck a chord with the foreign athletes.

In the early 2000s, Big Rock entered the acquisitions game, collecting three breweries: the Whistler Brewing Company and Bowen Island Brewing Company, both of BC, and Bear Brewing, of Alberta. Since then, Big Rock has refocused on its own brewing operations, divesting itself of each acquisition and instead building its portfolio of brands, which features nine different offerings straddling North American and international tastes, with everything from a low-calorie lager to a seven-percent ABV Irish ale.

Brick Brewing Company, Waterloo, Ontario

Toward the close of 1984, Waterloo, Ontario, joined the emerging craft-brew ranks when Jim Brickman founded the Brick Brewing Company. Brick Brewing has been the centre of much attention and beer controversy over its 25-year existence, and today it operates, without its founder, as Ontario's largest independent brewer.

For Brickman, the journey toward craft brewing started in 1978 with a four-year odyssey. Frustrated with trying to find a beer in Ontario that he could really enjoy, he set out with no brewing experience (and with the hope of gaining some) and toured 60 breweries across North America and Europe. When he returned to Canada, Brickman and his investors opened Ontario's first brewery in 37 years. Like McNally and Taylor, Brickman's first brew, Brick Premium Lager, complied with the Reinheitsgebot; it was officially available to the public on December 18, 1984, Brickman's birthday.

Since then, Brickman and Brick Brewing have made waves and grabbed headlines. In 1986 Brick Brewing became the first Canadian microbrewery to go public on the Toronto Stock Exchange; in 1996, Molson purchased a 12-percent interest in Brick Brewing while the company in turn inherited the Laker portfolio of brands from Molson; and in 1997, Brick Brewing purchased the struggling Algonquin Brewery. Along the way, Brick Brewing also bought the rights and recipe to an old Carling brew called Red Cap Ale. Red Cap was one of Carling's stronger brands in the 1950s and 1960s, but was long forgotten during the mega-merger days that typified Canadian brewing before the craft renaissance.

With Red Cap, Brickman grabbed hold of an opportunity to reconnect older drinkers with a brand full of sentiment and heritage. Inconspicuous in its 1994 launch, Red Cap was just another beer in the Brick Brewing portfolio, but in 2002, Brickman made the bold choice to go against the Industry Standard Bottle and instead packaged Red Cap in the long-defunct stubby. Brick Brewing's relaunch of the iconic brand in the iconic bottle had one big improvement: the replacement of the crown cap with the new twist-off standard.

The Red Cap stubby was a smash hit, and just as the big boys had reacted in the past, Molson, Labatt and Sleeman (the three brewers in charge of The Beer Store) took immediate offence to a product using the non-standard bottle. For a time, Brick Brewing's Red Cap was shut out of The Beer Store, and the store even threatened to withhold Industry Standard Bottles from Brick Brewing. Industry Standard Bottles were needed for the brewer's other brands, so Brick Brewing sued The Beer Store, and as a result, an injunction was passed allowing Brick Brewing into The Beer Store with the stubby bottle. The matter was finally settled out of court in 2008.

After six years of hoopla, in February 2009, Red Cap went back to the Industry Standard Bottle for cost-cutting reasons. The company felt that the extra sorting costs (close to $1 per case) charged by The Beer Store, plus line adjustments needed every time a Red Cap bottling cycle was due, incurred too much cost compared to the profitability of the brand. The same month the Red Cap bottle decision was announced, Brickman resigned from his own brewery. His departure came at a time when the company was looking to restructure and rebrand. The brewery dropped its award-winning and underappreciated J.R. Brickman line of beer and now revolves around the Waterloo Dark and Waterloo Wheat premium brands and the Ontario discount brands of Red Barron Lager, Red Cap Ale and the Laker series.

DID YOU  KNOW?

When Brick Brewing obtained the Laker brands from Molson in 1996, the brands they received in the acquisition were the Laker labels once owned by the Lakeport Brewing Company. Former Lakeport president Bill Sharpe sold the Laker brands to Molson in order to finance a buyout of his corporate partners. According to Allen Winn Sneath, Sharpe, having divested himself of his flagship Laker brand, created the Lakeport line of brews that Ontarians know today by using the same recipes he had used for Laker. The Lakeport Brewing Company was bought by foreign-owned Labatt in 2007, which continues to produce the Lakeport discount brand. The Laker brand (the original brand developed by Sharpe) is now a mainstay of the Brick Brewing line of beers. While most discount brands taste the same, consumers might be surprised to learn that these two brands sold by two different breweries—Labatt (Lakeport) and Brick (Laker)—are essentially identical.

Québec Steps Up to the Bar

Canada's burgeoning craft-beer segment didn't cross the borders of Québec until the mid-to-late 1980s, which might seem a little odd, considering that some of Canada's most internationally renowned beers now come from craft brewers in this province.

Massawipi Brewing Company and the Golden Lion Brewing Company, Lennoxville, Québec

The craft-brew story of Québec starts in Lennoxville, a small town just outside Sherbrooke. Lennoxville is home to Québec's first two brewpubs, both founded in 1986: the Massawipi Brewing Company and the Golden Lion Brewing Company.

The Massawipi Brewing Company didn't last long or fair well as a business, but its role in the Québec craft-brewing industry is undisputed, as it was purchased by André Dion in 1991 and became the first home for the much celebrated brewing company, Unibroue. The Golden Lion Brewing Company, whose creation was inspired after owner Stan Groves visited the Horseshoe Bay Brewery in the early 1980s, still exists, with a pub, café and brewery. Golden Lion serves its own beer and bottles select brews for sale in local convenience stores.

Le Cheval Blanc and Brasseurs GMT, Montréal, Québec
A third brewpub opened in the greater Montréal area in 1987. Known as the Le Cheval Blanc (which itself would go into full-scale brewing and bottling in 1995), this brewpub cemented the microbrew niche in Montréal and paved the way for the first full-scale craft brewery in Québec: Brasseurs GMT of Montréal. Brasseurs GMT (named after its founders Gilbert Gravel, André Martineau and Yves Thibault), like the Golden Lion, was inspired by a taste of West-coast thinking when the brewery's founding trio were introduced to the offerings produced by the Granville Island Brewery. The GMT threesome enlisted the help of brewmaster George Van Gheluwe, and in 1988, they kegged their first brew.

Le Cheval Blanc and Brasseurs GMT merged in 1998 with a third Québec brewery, Le Brasseurs de l'Anse Microbrewery, to form Les Brasseurs RJ, named after founding president, Roger Jaar. The present RJ brewery contains a portfolio of brands from each original brewery and also imports and distributes Tuborg and Carlsberg for the Québec market.

Les Brasseurs du Nord, Saint-Jérôme, Québec
In 1988, the influential Québec brewery Les Brasseurs du Nord got its start. Les Brasseurs du Nord, known for its Boréale line of beer, can actually trace its roots back to 1984 when its founders, as post-secondary students, brewed up

their own beer at home. The duo of Bernard Morin and Laura Urtnowski crafted a beer that was a hit with friends, and after Urtnowski obtained some practical training from the Wellington Brewery in Guelph, Ontario, she came back to Québec ready to start her own full-scale operation. And so, Urtnowski, along with Morin and his brother Jean, formed the trio who founded Les Brasseurs du Nord in Saint-Jérôme, Québec. Urtnowski's original, popular dark ale, Boréale Rousse, was the new company's first brew in June 1988.

Today, Les Brasseurs du Nord is the only Québec craft brewery wholly owned by its original founders. Its annual production of 70,000 hectolitres gives it a healthy one percent of the Québec beer market.

Brasserie McAuslan Brewing, Montréal, Québec

Also in 1988, Peter McAuslan and his wife and master brewer, Ellen Bounsall, began laying the groundwork for their own influential Montréal brewery, Brasserie McAuslan Brewing, with the help of British brewmaster Alan Pugsley. McAuslan, while first starting to formulate his interest in the craft-brew business, had met Pugsley at a craft-brew summit in Massachusetts in the mid-1980s. Pugsley helped guide the physical set-up of the couple's brewery and helped to refine the recipe process before he officially turned the duties over to his apprentice, Bounsall. Although construction of the brewery and the recipe for the first McAuslan ale (St-Ambroise Pale Ale) were complete by December 1988, Brasserie McAuslan didn't start producing its first batches of brew for sale until January 1989. The first kegs went out in February of that year, and by May, McAuslan-made beer was sold in bottles in pubs, restaurants and stores—making McAuslan the first craft brewery in Québec to have this distinction (the rest of the craft operators were only kegging their beer).

Brasserie McAuslan, who in 2000 sold a 45-percent stake of the company to Moosehead, is still controlled by Peter McAuslan. In 2008, Moosehead sold their 45-percent interest in McAuslan to Les Brasseurs RJ. Together, the two breweries, McAuslan and Brasseurs RJ, own five percent of the Québec beer market. McAuslan still produces the Moosehead brand for the Québec marketplace.

DID YOU  KNOW?

Both McAuslan and Unibroue have won platinum medals at the Beverage Testing Institute World Beer Championships. A platinum medal is awarded to a beer judged to exhibit superlative qualities in a specific beer class, as evaluated by world-leading beer tasters in a blind taste-test scenario. To record a superlative mark, a beer must receive a score of 96 or greater out of a possible 100 points. McAuslan succeeded in 1994 with their Oatmeal Stout, and most recently, in 2007, was awarded a score of 89 for the same brew, earning a silver medal. Unibroue was awarded a platinum medal in 2008 for its Belgian-style blonde ale, La Fin Du Monde, which scored a 96.

Kevin Keefe Starts a Revolution

Although at the forefront of traditional brewing in Canada, when it came to the craft-brew revolution, the Maritimes, with the exception of one man, got in on the action pretty late in the game. But by doing so, brew-aficionados-turned-brewmasters were able to learn from the rest of the country's mistakes. In fact, aside from Kevin Keefe who opened the Maritimes' first brewpub in 1985, the majority of the craft breweries and brewpubs that have opened since, and lasted, did so in the mid-to-late 1990s.

Keefe, the father of the East Coast craft-brewing renaissance, first opened his brewpub in Ginger's, the bar he and his brother, Wilfred, already owned and operated in Halifax. Ginger's was a reclamation project by the brothers 10 years earlier in 1975, when the two siblings took over what was a failing bar and grill. Three years after brewing commenced at Ginger's, the Keefes relocated their brewpub operations to a building on Barrington Street in the tourist harbourfront area of Halifax. The move was accompanied with a name change to the Granite Brewery.

Keefe wasn't a brewer by trade, so before he began his brewing career at the Ginger's location, he apprenticed at the

Ringwood Brewery in England with none other than Alan Pugsley, the same Pugsley who helped start the McAuslan brewery in Montréal in the late 1980s. It was at the Ringwood Brewery, however, where Keefe learned how to brew the distinctive English ales that the Granite Brewery is known for; it is also why the brewery uses Ringwood yeast in all its ales.

Keefe, a major player in the Halifax bar and restaurant industry for 34 years, closed the iconic Barrington Street brewpub in February 2009. The decision was made so Keefe could concentrate on the opening of his first full-scale brewery operation, a 9000-hectolitre facility in the northwest end of Halifax. Initial brew testing at the new facility began in April 2009, only a month removed from the shuttering of the brewpub. Keefe still has big ideas for Granite, however. He plans to open a 23,000-hectolitre facility in the Windsor, Nova Scotia, community of Mill Island, within the next few years.

DID YOU  KNOW?

Granite opened a Toronto location in 1991, making the family brewery not only Halifax's first brewpub, but Toronto's as well. The third brother of the Keefe clan, Ron, who made Toronto his home, had wanted nothing to do with the family restaurant/bar business until the concept of opening a brewpub in Toronto became a possibility. So Ron, with the help of his brother Kevin and brewery start-up expert, Alan Pugsley, opened the Granite Brewery in Toronto, at the corner of Mount Pleasant Avenue and Eglington Avenue. What started as a brewpub has since become a microbrewery with a restaurant. The distinction, according to Ontario law, allows Granite to sell the beer it produces not only at its restaurant, but also through other restaurants, bars and retail outlets.

AN INDUSTRY BEGINS TO GROW

Movin' On Up...

Between 1985 and 1995, the craft segment in Canada began to develop across the country. Every geographic region—from the West Coast to the Prairies to the East Coast—had developed at least one craft brewer or brewpub, and in a few instances, multiple operations were thriving in the same cities, let alone the same provinces.

This period was particularly fertile for the province of Ontario, whose population was witness to the rise of breweries such as the Upper Canada Brewing Company (1985), Wellington County Brewery (1985) and Creemore Springs Brewery (1987). The following for each brewery began with a cult-like status and has matured into mainstream acceptability. Upper Canada, concentrating on brew that conformed to the Reinheitsgebot, along with Wellington, whose cask-conditioned ales were the first of their kind in modern North American brewing, and Creemore, who stuck with one brand for their first nine years of business, helped the niche craft-beer segment gain sustainability. In Québec, this era saw the rise of one of Canada's most critically acclaimed breweries, Unibroue (1991), whose Belgian-influenced ales are the toast of many brewing awards and the beneficiary of much praise. The national breweries Labatt, Molson, Carling O'Keefe (which belonged to Molson come 1989), and later, Sleeman, started to take notice as the craft segment began to erode market-share points that were not easily won.

The Big Boys Come Out Swinging

"If you can't beat 'em, join 'em!" seemed to be the philosophy of Molson and Labatt in the mid-to-late 1990s, when, in reaction to the mounting pressure of the craft-brew segment, the two brewing giants responded with craft-like products of their own. For the big brewers, this was a time of new, mysterious, unidentifiable products and failed attempts at understanding the craft consumer. The result was a lot of wasted money, time and effort, and the recognition that the craft segment contained more than just a few hobbyists and anti-establishment types.

The line of products launched on the Canadian public by the Big Boys reads like a rap sheet. Courtesy of Molson: Molson Dry, Rickard's Red, Molson's Signature Series and Red Dog. Courtesy of Labatt: Labatt Genuine Draft, Duffy's Dark, Labatt Copper, Old Mick's Red, Kokanee and Alexander Keith's India Pale Ale. Only a few of these products still exist today, and the most noteworthy are Molson's Rickard's Red and the Labatt brand extensions of Kokanee and Alexander Keith's.

The difference between the two companies' surviving brands is that Rickard's Red was actually a new product released by Molson, while Kokanee and Alexander Keith's were regional beers that Labatt made into national products. What all three beers have in common is the deliberate omission, or masking, of the parent brewer on each product's identifiers: Rickard's first incarnation was as a beer brewed at the Capilano Brewing Company in BC, while Kokanee was billed as "BC's Mountain Beer." When the beers came to Ontario, both were produced in plants along Highway 401, not in BC; Rickard's Capilano name came from the BC brewery Molson purchased in 1959, which was renamed Molson Breweries Western Division in 1990. Alternately, Alexander Keith's was brewed in Nova Scotia and shipped across the country. It was never falsely represented as a beer brewed elsewhere, but that Alexander Keith's was first bought by the Oland family in 1928, and then acquired by Labatt in 1971, was lost on many people.

Today, Kokanee is a mainstream college beer, while Rickard's and Keith's are valuable brands with their own line extensions, such as Rickard's White and Keith's Amber Red Ale. Rickard's and Keith's are often dubbed "micro-killers" as their perceived status as craft-quality items allows bars and restaurants to charge more for the brews while paying less because Molson and Labatt award volume discounts to bars and restaurants that purchase large amounts of product.

"If you can't beat 'em, buy 'em out!"

If the Big Boys launching their own micro-killers wasn't enough of a blow to the tiny craft segment, the ebb and flow of mergers and acquisitions caught up with the craft brewers in the mid-to-late 1990s and the 2000s, creating a rift in the craft segment. Smaller breweries not only had to compete with the larger ones but also had to go up against one-time craft companies that now had access to big-company dollars.

Molson Buys Creemore Springs Brewery

The single biggest splash made by a large brewer in the craft segment happened in 2005 when Molson surprised many by taking over the Creemore Springs Brewery, which only had two brands at the time. The initial brand, Creemore Springs Premium Lager, which stood alone for almost a decade as the company's sole product, was the talk of the town for many years. Before Creemore founder John Wiggins would give his approval to any given pub to sell his Creemore lager, he personally visited each vendor in question. Subsequently, a waiting list was created that became beer legend—who ever heard of a brewery that made clients wait? It wasn't until years after The List ceased that a seasonal offering called UrBock joined the Premium Lager in 1996.

On the whole, not much has changed for Creemore since its merger with Molson. Creemore doesn't participate in more than print advertising (if at all) and still produces its beer in the Ontario town of its namesake. Even when the brewer decided to go to cans, a new canning operation was installed at the Creemore brewery as opposed to shipping the beer to a larger Molson plant for canning. Beer insiders do, however, lament the loss of the company's 500-millilitre bottle, changed for sorting regulations at The Beer Store. The biggest movement for Creemore since its Molson merger was the introduction of Creemore Springs Traditional Pilsner in 2007 to celebrate the company's 20th anniversary of brewing in Creemore.

Sleeman's Expansion

So while Molson did provide the biggest *single* splash by a large brewer in the craft segment, Sleeman, formerly a craft start-up, created the largest shakeup. The family brewery, relaunched in 1988 by John W. Sleeman, quickly shot up the ladder to major-player status in the late '80s and early '90s, facilitated by the string of mergers and acquisitions orchestrated by the new family brewing patriarch. The first buyout on Sleeman's watch was the Okanagan Spring Brewery of Vernon, BC, in 1996. Next, Sleeman purchased the empty Drummond Brewery of Red Deer, Alberta, in 1997, and then in 1998, for what some considered an underpriced bid, Sleeman purchased Toronto's first craft brewery, the Upper Canada Brewing Company. The Upper Canada plant was closed shortly after, and production was moved to the Sleeman facilities in Guelph. Sleeman continued to plow across the country, setting up shop in Québec with the purchase of La Brasserie Seigneuriale of Boucherville in 1998 and completing his cross-country shopping tour with the buyout of the Maritime Beer Company of Dartmouth, Nova Scotia, in 2000. Within four years, Sleeman had leapfrogged Moosehead and became the country's third-largest brewer—but John W. wasn't finished. Having already purchased a second BC brewer in 1999, the Shaftebury Brewing Company, Sleeman decided to further fortify his position in Québec with the takeover of Unibroue in 2004.

For the most part, Sleeman's brewery expansion was done in order to gain unfettered access to each province's retail sector, so as to avoid paying interprovincial taxes and levies assigned to brewers who wished to sell their suds in a province outside of their home brewing location. For those brewers taken over by Sleeman, however, the majority of their original lineups are still available, with little or no changes. This mode of takeover is a refreshing change from the hack-and-slash brand management of men like E.P. Taylor. That being said, some breweries, like Upper Canada, had more significant changes forced upon them by Sleeman, leaving many fans of the former Toronto brewer less than satisfied with the current state of Upper Canada offerings.

In 2006, Sapporo Breweries Limited of Japan took control of Sleeman. It still remains to be seen what changes, if any, the new owners of Sleeman will impose on the regional lineup.

DID YOU  KNOW?

The Drummond Brewery of Red Deer, Alberta, was reopened in 2008. Well, *reopened* is not necessarily correct, as the brewery didn't open at the same site purchased by Sleeman in 1997. Instead, Kevin Wood and Cody Geddes-Backman opened a new brewery in Red Deer at 6610-71 Street. The name "Drummond Brewery" belonged to Sleeman, but the national brewer allowed the name's trademark to lapse. With no one claiming ownership of the Drummond Brewery trademark name, Wood and Geddes-Backman were able to obtain it and reappropriate a little bit of Red Deer history. In a conversation about the new brewery with the *Red Deer Advocate*, Wood said, "John Sleeman was a little surprised when I joined the Brewers Association." The Drummond Brewery currently boasts two products, Drummond Premium Lager and Drummond Gold, an amber lager.

IT KEEPS GOING AND GOING...

The Resurrection

Between 1995 and 1997, the craft-brewing scene on the East Coast exploded, with no less than six influential breweries beginning operations and at least one brewery located in each province. The Maritimes hadn't seen this kind of boom since Canada's first wave of brewers got brewing over 100 years earlier.

Storm Brewing

Newfoundland and New Brunswick claimed the first two brewing operations, with the Freshwater Brewing Company of Carbonear, Newfoundland, and the Picaroon's Brewing Company of Fredericton, New Brunswick, launching in 1995. Freshwater relocated its brewery to St. John's in 1997, and in 1999 changed its name to Storm Brewing, by which it is still known. Today, Storm Brewing has a portfolio of five ales coming from its small seven-hectolitre facility. Storm's ales range from standard reds and golds to the specialty offerings of Coffee Porter, Raspberry Wheat Ale and Hemp Ale. Picaroon's currently has 11 ales, ranging in style from Irish stout to English bitter and porter, to the very Canadian, Maple Cream Ale.

Quidi Vidi Brewing Company

Newfoundland's second craft operation—the Quidi Vidi Brewing Company of Quidi Vidi—opened in 1996 with one brew, 1892 Traditional Ale. In the years since 1996, Quidi Vidi has grown to an eight-brew portfolio, with a moderately mainstream feel. The brewery produces North American-style lagers and low-calorie lagers, along with honey offerings in

both light and regular. Its most interesting product is its Iceberg Beer, which it brews as a light-tasting lager with iceberg water that the company harvests itself.

Garrison Brewing and the Propeller Brewing Company
Halifax's Garrison Brewing and the Propeller Brewing Company both opened in 1997. The two brewers are multiple medal winners at the Canadian Brewing Awards, and both produce fine English ales and wheat selections. Garrison, specifically, produces an arsenal of specialty brews, including Moka Ale and the ever-interesting Jalapeño Ale.

Gahan Brewery

The first incarnation of Prince Edward Island's only craft
brewery/brewpub, the Gahan House, opened in 1997 as the
Lone Star Brewery, which took its name from its location, the
Tex-Mex chain restaurant, Lone Star. Leaving the original
Lone Star location and moniker behind, the brewery changed
its name to Murphy's Brewing Company (after owner, Kevin
Murphy), and upon a second relocation in 2000 to the heritage
Gahan House, the company changed its name to the Gahan
Brewery. As the only PEI brewery, Gahan Brewery offers
seven different brews, the majority of which are created in the
English style.

DID YOU  KNOW?

Storm Brewing is influential throughout Newfoundland and
the Canadian brewing industry because of its status as
Canada's first zero-emissions brewery. At Storm, mushrooms
are grown from waste barley, and worms are added to the
resulting compost to eat the leftover nutrients, leaving
the once-spent barley mash as high-nitrogen garden fertilizer
(vermicompost). Most breweries give their waste barley to
farmers as cattle feed, but this is inefficient as the inability of
cattle to break down the barley properly results in excess
methane gas in the air.

 Storm Brewing in Newfoundland is not
to be confused with Storm Brewing of
Vancouver, also founded in 1995. Storm
Brewing of Vancouver has anywhere from
five to eight varieties of beer on its list
(depending on the availability of its selection of fruit
Lambics), including the celebrated Hurricane IPA

EXTREME BREWING

In North America, the use of specialty ingredients and processes has paved the way for the concept of extreme craft-brewing. As Sam Calagione, the founder of Dogfish Head Brewery in Milton, Delaware, likes to say, extreme brewing is beer "made with extreme amounts of traditional ingredients or beers made extremely well with non-traditional ingredients." Calagione is often credited with inciting a revolution in North American brewing, but he is quick to point out that extreme brewing didn't just happen, it has been in the works for centuries—from Belgian monks to North American craft brewers. The following are a few particularly outstanding examples of extreme craft-brews, the first made by the inspired Calagione.

Midas Touch

This beer-wine-mead concoction (mead is an alcoholic beverage made with honey) was made in 1999 for the recreation of the King Midas Feast at the University of Pennsylvania in Philadelphia. The university was attempting to recapture the feast left in the 2700-year-old tomb believed to belong to King Midas. In ancient times, when a person died, it was customary to outfit their tomb with all they would need for survival in the afterlife, and this supply included food and drink. In the case of royalty, no expense was spared in providing the best people had to offer for the regal tomb.

Molecular archaeologist Patrick McGovern analyzed the residue left in shards of beer pottery found in the King Midas tomb in Turkey and discovered a 2700-year-old brew made from white grapes, thyme, honey and barley. McGovern sought out Dogfish Head and asked them to recreate the recipe for the feast at the University of Pennsylvania. With little trepidation, Calagione and his team accepted the challenge and went to work.

The result was a smooth and sweet honey ale with the dryness of white wine. The tasting notes on the Dogfish Head website list honey, saffron, papaya, melon, biscuity and succulent as flavours and terms describing the beer, while other tasters have mentioned sweet apple and ice-wine-like sweetness.

Midas Touch is a decidedly decadent beer originally brewed for an individual whom the history books have described as a decidedly decadent man.

King Tut's Tipple

Brewed in 2004 by Spinnakers Brewpub in Victoria, BC, for the Eternal Egypt exhibit that made its stop at the Royal British Columbia Museum, King Tut's Tipple was inspired by a 3250-year-old Egyptian recipe first unearthed in the mid-1990s by Delwen Samuel of the University of Cambridge.

The recipe Samuel reconstructed—from residue found in beer pottery shards and hieroglyphics depicting the process used to make the beer—featured fermented barley and emmer (an ancient wheat that hadn't been produced for nearly 2000 years). Juniper and coriander were also employed, as was a local berry called naback. The first brewer to make a version of this ale was the British brewer Scottish & Newcastle, which, in 1996, released a limited-run stock (1000 bottles) of the now famous Tutankhamen Ale. The beer debuted with much fanfare and publicity, and bottles numbered 2 to 1000 sold at Harrods of London for £50 a pop (approximately C$89). Upping that price considerably, bottle number one sold for a reported £5000 (approximately C$8896)! Proceeds from the sale of the beer went to fund further Egyptian archeological exploration.

Spinnakers' version of this royal ale, King Tut's Tipple, was also a limited-time-only brew. Spinnakers, well known for its fine craftsmanship and exciting creations, coupled its Egyptian brew with an Egyptian-themed menu in its award-winning restaurant. The Tipple was brewed with locally grown heritage emmer and flavoured with fig and star anise instead of juniper and coriander. The resulting taste was sweet and tart with a dry, white-wine-like finish. King Tut's Tipple was produced through to the end of 2004, and Spinnakers continues to make some very impressive ales and lagers with a great portfolio of internationally inspired choices.

Holy Smoke Scotch Ale

A personal favourite, Holy Smoke Scotch Ale is produced by one of Ontario's best and most unique craft-breweries, Church-Key Brewing of Pethrick's Corners, just outside Campbellford. The brewery, which runs out of a late 19th-century Methodist church, has a trio of brews offered year-round, supplemented by a bevy of seasonal favourites, including Cranberry Maple Wheat Ale and Ginger Rosemary Spiced Ale.

Holy Smoke Scotch Ale, a gold-medal winner at the Canadian Brewing Awards in 2003 and 2004, is a major-league Scotch ale. Deep, dark brown—almost black—this ale subverts the norm for Scotch-ale alcohol content (which is usually low) with an ABV of 6.25 percent. The brew is medium-bodied with a healthy malt flavour and little hop taste. The aroma is that of barbecue, bacon and smoked peat. I've actually heard it described as liquid barbecue! The smoky flavour and aroma are the result of imported Scottish smoked whiskey malt.

Maltitude Russian Imperial Stout

The pride of the New Brunswick craft-brewing scene is 2005 Canadian Brewery of the Year winner, The Pump House Brewery of Moncton. Started as a brewpub in 1999, the business has grown to include a brewery and a bottling plant, as well as an on-site restaurant.

With an ABV of 10 percent, Maltitude Russian Imperial Stout is a big beer. Typically, Russian Imperial stouts are high-alcohol content, dark, hoppy brews. When the English and Russian courts traded in the 1800s, English brewers sent stout to Russia. In order for the stout to make the trip unspoiled, the brewers added extra hops and let the beer finish fermenting en route. Maltitude is less hoppy than other Russian Imperials and instead has the added elements of fresh, locally roasted espresso beans, peated malt and demerara sugar. The resulting brew is full-bodied with a smoky character and notes of chocolate and coffee in the finish.

The Pump House also features eight all-year brews and just as many seasonal selections. Popular choices are Fire Chief Red Ale, Scotch Ale and the unique Blueberry Ale.

Other Extreme Favourites

- Jalapeño Ale, Garrison Brewing, Halifax, Nova Scotia

- Blackberry Mead, Bushwakker Brewing Company, Regina, Saskatchewan

- Dementia Double IPA, Pump House Brewery Ltd., Moncton, New Brunswick

- Special Edition Uniek Sour Cherry Ale, Better Bitters Brewing Company, Burlington, Ontario

- Green Tea Ale, Great Lakes Brewing Company, Toronto, Ontario

CANADA'S BEST CRAFT-BREW CITY

There is a lot of talk about where it is best to quaff craft brew in Canada. Some say Canada's culture capital, Montréal, is the place to be. With its wide variety of award-winning Belgian-, English- and North American-style beers, Montréal creates a strong argument for itself. Add in the city's vibrant bar scene and award-winning brewpubs, and Montréal seems like the top choice. Others, however, say you need to go to the East Coast to experience Canada's best brew. With their wide variety of English-style ales, mixed with solid offerings of German and Belgian favourites, it, too, is a good pick. And then there is Canada's favourite city, Toronto, which might possibly lead the Canadian craft-brew segment in quality and quantity. With multiple award-winning brews and larger distribution networks, along with some worldly small-town Ontario beers joining in the mix, Toronto makes a strong case for the unofficial award of Canada's craft crown.

But the province to start it all, BC, and its capital, Victoria, take the cake. With a population just shy of 350,000, the Victoria area has four brewpubs—Spinnakers, Swans, Canoe and Hugo's Brewhouse—and also boasts four craft breweries. From the pioneering Vancouver Island Brewery (1984) to the new Driftwood Brewery (2008) to the simple Lighthouse Brewery (1998) to the complex Phillips Brewery (2001), Victoria can no doubt claim unrivalled rights to the Canadian craft-brew crown.

The small-scale Lighthouse Brewery brews but four drinkable, classic styles: premium lager, amber ale, India pale ale and stout. Phillips, on the other hand, boasts 16 eclectic styles of beer—everything from a chocolate porter to a double India pale ale to a Belgian triple. And if none of these examples suit your tastes, just take a walk, because together, the brewpubs and breweries of Victoria combine for over 75 distinct brews (give or take, depending on the season).

The Victoria brewpubs not only include the oldest brewpub in Canada (Spinnakers) but both it and Swans are also Canadian pioneers in another regard. Each of these brew-pubs features resort-style accommodations to accompany their other amenities. At Swans, guests can have their pints delivered by room service! What's more is that Spinnakers and Swans (and Canoe) bottle their most popular brands for sale at off-site liquor marts across the city. If all of Victoria's choices are overwhelming, sleep on it. You can order a beer brought to your room when you wake up!

THE BEER MANUAL

A manual for Canadian beer? *Yes!* Isn't it time to take the one thing you're really good at—drinking beer—and shape it into something formidable? Something sublime? Keg stands and beer pong will still have their place, but now is your chance to push beyond the boundaries defined by commercials and lame beer rhetoric and educate yourself about the splendid potent potable, to which I'm sure you owe much in this life. Cracking open a cold one on a hot summer day or enjoying a few wobbly-pops with the boys while watching *Hockey Night in Canada* are great pastimes and pillars of the Canadian beer-drinking community, but there is more to the beer-drinker's life than that!

The following are six simple steps (some are *really* simple) that will not only allow you to appreciate beer that much more, but will also leave you full of knowledge and under-standing about how Canadians across the country have shared, and do share, in the same pastime you do.

Touching, isn't it? To borrow an oft-used expression, which I think means that you are ready for the finer things in life, "Welcome to your Carlsberg years."

STEP 1: PURCHASING YOUR BEER

For those forward-thinking types who already have reserves of their own homebrew, great. For the rest of us, however, in order to enjoy beer, we first have to obtain it. Outside of the pub or brewery, this is done in a different way in each province and territory.

BC

If you want to pick up a few cold brewskies for your trip to Whistler on the weekend, you have three options in BC's mixed public-private beverage-alcohol retail model: licensee retail stores, government-run liquor stores and rural agency stores.

Licensee stores are the most ubiquitous purveyors of beer in BC, as the province has almost 700 licensed, privately owned stores.

Each licensee store is attached to a liquor-primary business (bar, pub, etc.) and can be open anywhere from 9:00 AM to 11:00 PM. So if you are out with the boys to watch the hockey game and want a few cold ones for when you get home, just slip on into the retail store before you leave the bar. What's more is that licensee stores can deliver! There is absolutely nothing like getting both pizza and beer without having to get up off the couch. NOTHING.

Unfortunately, while these stores are subject to minimum provincial prices for beer, they aren't subject to any kind of maximum price. This system sets up a double-edged sword: with a concentration of stores in a small area, prices will most

likely be competitive, but if a store is the last one on the way out of town, or the only store in a tourist or rural area, there is nothing stopping the retailer from selling what would normally be bargain beer for premium beer prices—and that ain't cool.

The government-run liquor stores, or BC Liquor Stores as they are called, aren't hard to find, either, as the province has 197 of them. The prices are the same from store to store, and that is handy to know when you're down on your luck and in definite need of some suds. Some stores may have more to offer than others, but by and large, the selection is acceptable. If you are an über-crazed beer aficionado and must have a bottle of a rare seasonal brew, the BC Liquor Stores' website (bcliquorstores.com) has a searchable database of products—you can even conduct your search by store. For those of you who want the Molson Canadian, it's down the third aisle, left-hand side.

Your last option in BC is 227 rural agency stores, and for many people, this is their first and only option. Rural agency stores are located in communities that are too small to have a BC Liquor Store and too far away from another community that has a liquor store—talk about "out there." The selection at rural stores may not be the best because they function as a foodstuffs store first and liquor outlet second. Prices charged at rural agency stores are in line with those charged at BC Liquor Stores, but a rural location is allowed to charge a "chill fee" for refrigerated beverages.

Price check: Average price in BC for 24 premium domestic beer: $39, taxes included.

Alberta

The only province in Canada to have a completely privatized liquor industry, Alberta might just be the greatest place in Canada to buy booze—then again, it might not be. Sixteen years have gone by since the government sold its interest in the liquor business, and from September 1993 to today, the number of retail liquor outlets in Alberta has grown from 803 to 1707; that is 447 more retail outlets than in the province of Ontario!

In reality, the population of Alberta, like in most other Canadian provinces, is spread out, with the majority of liquor retailers residing in the larger urban centres. In a rural community where there is only one place to purchase beer, that private retailer's monopoly on the industry in that one community can create a distinct disadvantage for the consumer. A market run by private industry can set prices to whatever it feels the market can bear. Stated in section four of the Alberta Gaming and Liquor Commission's guide to operating a retail liquor store is:

> *4.1.1 Retail liquor stores may set their own retail prices. Consumer response and market forces will influence pricing.*

> *4.4.2 Retail liquor stores may adjust prices based on the customer, the amount of sale or any factor deemed relevant, at the discretion of the retail liquor store operator.*

Needless to say, buying beer in Alberta might be really cheap or really expensive. Let's just hope for your sake that there aren't any supplier strikes, heat waves or general beer shortages.

But enough of that. You want to get your beer, right? Well, with close to 2000 places to choose from, finding beer won't be hard; in fact, to make it easier for you the Alberta Gaming and Liquor Commission allows vendors to deliver beer; moreover, retail vendors can sell beer online! So not only can you stay home, you also don't have to talk to anyone if you don't want to. Of course, deliveries will cost you more than getting up and going to the store yourself, as it is mandatory for retailers to charge a delivery fee. The Alberta Gaming and Liquor Commission stops short of allowing outright virtual retail, though, as anyone selling beer online must also operate a physical store. And for you night owls, you can legally purchase beer for home consumption until 2:00 AM.

Price check: Average price in Alberta for 24 premium domestic beer: N/A (because of the privatization of the liquor industry here, pricing is not consistent across the board). It is worthy to note, however, that in a study by the Canadian Mental Health Association on the privatization of the Alberta liquor industry, the average price of alcohol increased 8.5 percent in the first two and a half years after privatization.

Saskatchewan

Outside of Québec, Saskatchewan boasts the highest per-capita rate of liquor outlets to legal drinking-age population, with a ratio of close to one outlet for every 1000 citizens. The division of liquor retailers is split with 264 government-run stores and licensees and 463 "off-site," privately owned retailers. Retailers are deemed "off-site" because they allow consumers to purchase alcohol to drink at home—hence, off-site—as opposed to "on-site" private retailers, such as bars and clubs, that allow you to drink at the location where you have purchased your drink.

Purchasing beer is a possibility at all 727 retail outlets, but your options are limited depending on where you choose to shop.

Of the 264 government-run retailers, 79 are full-fledged liquor stores that offer a wide variety of wine, spirits and domestic and import brews; the remaining 185 retailers are known as franchise stores, which range from convenience stores to pharmacies to hardware stores. Franchise stores operate in more rural locales, offering wine and spirits, but only imported beer. The best place to get your beer in Saskatchewan is at an off-site store, which operates attached to hotels, brewpubs and bars. These places not only provide the biggest supply of domestic beer, they also supply it chilled—something not routine for government-run stores.

All retailers are subject to minimum prices set by the Saskatchewan Liquor and Gaming Authority, but private off-site purveyors of chilled brewskies are free to set their own beer markups. The saving grace for beer consumers in Saskatchewan is that with set-priced beer available across the province, private retailers will more than likely price their brews competitively.

 Price check: Average price in Saskatchewan for 24 premium domestic beer: $39, taxes included.

Manitoba

Manitobans get their beer for home consumption in one of three ways: the Liquor Mart, a liquor vendor or a beer vendor.

For Manitobans, going to a Liquor Mart means going to the "LC." The LC is short for the MLCC, or the Manitoba Liquor Control Commission. There are 48 Liquor Mart stores throughout Manitoba, and every single one of them sells beer—generally, the larger the store, the larger the beer selection. The MLCC Liquor Marts display their products online, but it is a system-wide database and is not geared for store-by-store shopping. That being said, the MLCC will home-deliver beer with a just a phone call, but beware: if you want your suds the same day, you'll have to order them by 1:00 PM.

Liquor vendors operate in communities that are too small for a stand-alone Liquor Mart. In a province full of rural communities, it is no surprise that there are almost four times as many liquor vendors in Manitoba than there are Liquor

Marts. The liquor vendors, under licence from the MLCC, operate just like a Liquor Mart and charge standard Liquor Mart prices. The town grocer is often where you'll find a liquor vendor, and because of this, space can be limited for booze—which means beer selection is often minimal.

There are 175 liquor vendors in Manitoba, but this number doesn't yet represent the largest number of retail spaces in the province that are devoted to potent potables. It pretty much goes without saying that if you're buying beer in Manitoba, you're going to do so from one of the province's 278 beer vendors. A beer vendor cannot be a stand-alone business and must be attached to a hotel, motel or an inn—perfect for those overnight stays in Elphinstone!

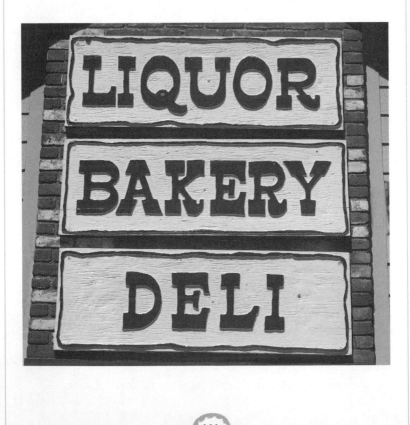

Price check: Average price in Manitoba for 24 premium domestic beer: $38, taxes included.

Ontario

At first, it seems so simple. If you want to purchase beer in Ontario, you go to The Beer Store; it is where the beers are, after all.

But The Beer Store isn't what many people think it is.

If you never asked any questions, you could easily assume that The Beer Store is a government-run store, operating much the same way the Liquor Control Board of Ontario (LCBO) outlets do. But neither of these things are true. In fact, The Beer Store is a private enterprise run by the three largest brewers in Ontario: Labatt, Molson and Sleeman— and none of these brewers are fully Canadian-owned, which means that foreign interests are earning nearly $1 billion per year from Ontario beer drinkers. Further compounding the issue is that outside of The Beer Store, the only other privately owned beer-vending outlets the Alcohol and Gaming Commission of Ontario will sanction are those attached to a brewery (in which the brewery can only sell its brands), thus giving The Beer Store a stranglehold on the Ontario beer market. The Ontario Convenience Stores Association has lobbied the provincial government numerous times for the right to sell beer in its stores, but the association contin-ues to get turned down for a litany of reasons ranging from the difficulty of policing such a system to the potential impact on minors of having beer on convenience store shelves.

So until 7–11 can serve beer in Ontario, you can, for the most part, purchase your brewskies for home consumption in one of two places: The Beer Store or the LCBO.

The Beer Store has by far the largest selection, as it houses over 350 varieties of beer produced by 80 companies. There are also 440 locations, each differing in size, layout and product availability. Because each one of the 80 represented brewers can choose which stores it would like to stock its product in, regional tastes can drastically vary what is available from one store to another. What can be said of all Beer Stores is that there is no shortage, of course, of Molson, Labatt or Sleeman products. A nice touch for consumers, however, is that 90 percent of the time, the beer you purchase is stored cold and therefore sold cold (some older stores still have non-chilled floor shelving space, but this is rare).

The LCBO, meanwhile, has a smaller but still impressive selection of beer, mostly consisting of imports and Ontario microbrews. Ontario's liquor store has 604 retail outlets and 216 rural agency stores; agency stores operate in communities too small for a large-scale government store and, like most other agency stores in other provinces, exist inside another store. Space is limited and so is selection, but hey, you can still get your beer.

As one last option for Ontarians seeking out the suds, it might be useful to know that entrepreneurs can apply through the AGCO for a Liquor Delivery Licence. These third-party agencies deliver booze to Ontario residences for a fee and have the option to deliver goods from both The Beer Store and the LCBO.

 Price check: Average price in Ontario for 24 premium domestic beer: $37, taxes included.

Québec

A Québecois bachelor grocery list might look something like this: macaroni and cheese, potato chips, frozen meals, bananas, toilet paper, beer.

You'll notice that beer made the bachelor's list for things to purchase at the grocery store. That's because in Québec, residents have the luxury of buying their domestic beer from grocery stores and convenience stores (dépanneurs). In fact, the province's government-run agency, the SAQ (Société des alcools du Québec), which has 414 outlets, only sells imported beer.

In order for a grocery or convenience store to sell beer, the retailer must have 51 percent of its floor space dedicated to foodstuffs. Beer can be sold from 8:00 AM to 11:00 PM and is subject to government minimum prices that vary by bottle volume. The lowest possible price is $0.81 for a 330-millilitre bottle of beer rating at 4.1-percent ABV or below; the highest minimum price is $3.40 for a 1.18-litre bottle of beer rating at 6.2-percent ABV and above. (Beer of five-percent ABV issued in the Industry Standard Bottle checks in at a minimum price of $0.95 per bottle, or $5.71 for six.) With minimum prices so low, retailers near provincial borders are often busy with traffic from neighbouring out-of-province communities. Many Québec retailers offer weekend-sale pricing to make the trip for outsiders that much more lucrative.

 Price check: Average price in Québec for 24 premium domestic beer: $27, taxes included.

Newfoundland

If you buy beer in Newfoundland and Labrador, you are purchasing beer from the Newfoundland Labrador Liquor Corporation (NLC), the government body that controls the sale of all alcohol in the province.

The NLC operates 25 full-service NLC Liquor Stores and 120 Liquor Express stores. Both stores offer beer products for home consumption and operate much the same as their brethren across the country: NLC Liquor Stores operate in more population-dense areas, and the Liquor Express stores function in communities too small for a full-service store. As far as beer selection is concerned, the general rule can be applied that the bigger the store, the better the selection. Regardless of venue, prices remain the same throughout the province.

The other (and most popular) option for purchasing beer in Newfoundland and Labrador is what the NLC calls brewer's agents. A brewer's agent is a private enterprise, like a convenience store, that the NCL has appointed to sell beer—and only beer—to the public. These retailers are required to operate under the auspices of the NLC, and they must charge the same price as liquor stores and express marts. What makes brewer's agents so popular is that they can only stock domestic beer that is bottled and distributed within the province. You won't find imports at a brewer's agent store, but you will find chilled local products, and that's nice. Plus, the province has over 1100 brewer's agent locations to choose from.

Price check: Average price in Newfoundland for 24 premium domestic beer: $41, taxes included.

Nova Scotia

Nova Scotia good times can only be purchased through the Nova Scotia Liquor Corporation (NSLC): a Crown corporation responsible for beverage-alcohol distribution and sales.

It goes without saying that, like most government-run liquor operations in Canada, the NSLC has two versions of its controlled distribution method: NSLC Liquor Stores—large, well-stocked retail outlets for all types of alcohol including beer—and rural agency stores, which operate in communities too small for a full-service NSLC Liquor Store.

In total, the NSLC has 162 outlets: 106 full-service stores and 56 rural agency locations. Agency stores are typically convenience-type stores that can offer any product sold at an NSLC store. Each proprietor decides which products to sell within its agency store, but anything it does sell is priced identically to products in an NSLC Liquor Store.

Since 2007, beer consumers in Nova Scotia might have noticed more out-of-province brews on the shelves at NSLC Liquor Stores. This is because new agreements between Nova Scotia and the provinces of New Brunswick and Québec have lightened the levies assessed to beer sold in Nova Scotia from these two provinces. The same can be said of Nova Scotia brews, which are now more readily available at lower prices in both New Brunswick and Québec.

Price check: Average price in Nova Scotia for 24 premium domestic beer: $39, taxes included.

New Brunswick

Alcool New Brunswick Liquor (ANBL) operates much like the NSLC in Nova Scotia. The Crown corporation is responsible for all beverage-alcohol purchases, distribution and sales within New Brunswick and operates both full-service and agency stores. New Brunswick currently boasts 46 retail stores and 73 licensed-retail partners. Retail partner stores are operated in communities too small to support a full-service ANBL outlet and are commonly found in convenience stores.

Both agency stores and ANBL full-service stores offer chilled beer, and 38 of the 46 ANBL Liquor Stores have a "chill room," where customers will find the store's entire beer selection.

On March 12, 2009, the ANBL launched a campaign unique to Canada: they released their own private-label domestic beer, making them the first liquor board in Canada to offer its own beer to the public. The ANBL's two brands, Selection Lager and Selection Light, are brewed under contract by Moosehead Breweries of New Brunswick. The concept for the private-label beer was born of the need for a local discount-beer option to slow the trend of out-of-province beer shopping. New Brunswickers can routinely find lower-cost beer in the bordering provinces of Québec and Nova Scotia and the U.S. state of Maine. For 12 cans of the 355-millilitre size, both Selection Lager and Selection Light retail for $18.67.

Price check: Average price in New Brunswick for 24 premium domestic beer: $40, taxes included.

Prince Edward Island

As the least-populated province in Canada, it is no surprise that the Prince Edward Island Liquor Control Commission (PEILCC) also has the smallest amount of retail space when compared to its provincial counterparts. The PEILCC, which controls all beverage-alcohol purchases, distribution and sales within the province, runs 19 full-service liquor stores and only one rural agency store. Many of the liquor-store locations in PEI offer chilled beer, and all locations throughout the province operate on the same price scale. Oh, and Islanders can now get their beer in cans, if they so choose. (You may remember that the province had a "can ban" on beer since 1973 and canned pop since 1984, which in turn meant that everything until 2008 was sold in a bottle. Imagine, a whole province full of people who have never shotgunned a beer.)

Price check: Average price in Prince Edward Island for 24 premium domestic beers: $40, taxes included.

DID YOU  KNOW?

Shotgunning a beer is akin to funnelling beer—it is a super-quick way to down a cold one. In order to shotgun a beer, you'll need a full, unopened beer can (do not use good beer for this!). While holding the can horizontally, puncture the can toward the bottom with a sharp object (key, bottle opener, knife). Keeping the can horizontal, quickly put your mouth over the hole you just created. Now, turn the can upright, get ready and open the tab at the top of the can. As the can's pressure is released with the tab opening, the beer will shoot out of the hole in the bottom of the can. I haven't clocked it, but a 355-millilitre can should be empty in about three seconds.

Northwest Territories

Consumers can purchase beer for home consumption in the Northwest Territories from seven government-run liquor stores and six off-site licence holders. The liquor system in the Northwest Territories is set up much like that of the Manitoba Liquor Control Commission. The Northwest Territories Liquor Commission (NWTLC) is responsible for the purchase, sale and distribution of liquor throughout its territory. Like the MLCC, the NWTLC allows proprietors of hotels, motels and inns the opportunity to operate an off-site store, as long as the store is in a community that doesn't already have a full-service liquor store.

Where the liquor industry differs in the Northwest Territories from its provincial and territorial counterparts is in its practice of helping communities exercise liquor-purchasing minimums and maximums within "restricted" alcohol-consumption parameters. Every community in the Northwest Territories has the power to determine the liquor status of their community by holding a liquor plebiscite, with a 60-percent vote in favour of whatever change is proposed. As a result, the sale of liquor in 11 communities in the Northwest Territories is under strict guidelines. Each community has its own regulations, but many of the restrictions focus on the amount of alcohol a citizen of the community is allowed to purchase within a given amount of time. Currently, of the 11 restricted communities, two have restrictions on what can be purchased by an individual inside one month; four have restrictions on what can be purchased by an individual inside seven days; and five have restrictions on what can be purchased by an individual inside 24 hours. As far as off-site stores are concerned, no matter what community they are located in, they are only permitted to sell a minimum of six bottles or cans and a maximum of 12 bottles or cans to any individual in a 24-hour period.

The NWTLC has also helped to exercise outright bans on alcohol in six alcohol-prohibited communities.

 Price check: Average price in the Northwest Territories for 24 premium domestic beer: $52, taxes included.

Yukon

The Yukon has the most liquor-based retail of all the territories. The Yukon Liquor Corporation (YLC) is responsible for the purchase, sale and distribution of all alcohol in the territory, and while the territory has six government-run liquor outlets, compared to the Northwest Territories' seven, the Yukon possesses a total of 23 off-site liquor vendors, 17 more than the Northwest Territories Liquor Commission oversees.

The Yukon's flagship government-run store in Whitehorse is strictly an alcohol retailer, while the remaining five are positioned as Territorial Agents. Agent stores act on behalf of the government to not only sell alcohol but also to administer a variety of licences and permits.

The 23 off-site locations can stock any item carried by the YLC and are permitted to charge a markup to a maximum of 30 percent higher than the YLC's base prices.

 Price check: Average price in the Yukon for 24 premium domestic beer: $39, taxes included.

Nunavut

Getting beer in Nunavut is an experience like no other you'll have in Canada. The reason being that the 10-year-old territory, home to almost 30,000 people, does not have a retail outlet for over-the-counter alcohol shopping. You can get alcohol in Nunavut, it just takes some planning.

So you find yourself in Nunavut and you want to toss back a few cold ones in the comfort of your home. What do you do? Well, there are two options to curb your craving. If you're in Iqaluit or Rankin Inlet and would like to purchase some beer, you'll need to head down to the Nunavut Liquor Commission's office, place an order and pay for it. After payment, your order gets collected and then delivered to you, most often by air freight. In the best-case scenario, you'll have your beer the same day you purchased it; worst-case scenario, you'll have your brew 72 hours from when you ordered it.

If you live outside Iqaluit or Rankin Inlet, you first have to get your order approved by the Alcohol Education Committee. Once approval is granted, a wireless transaction for funds is made and your order is shipped.

Your other option in obtaining beer is to go outside of Nunavut and make your purchases in places like Yellowknife or Churchill—essentially in cities Nunavut locals refer to as "down south." In order to have beer, or any alcohol, brought into Nunavut from another province or territory, you need to obtain an import permit. To get a permit, you can visit the NLC's offices in Iqaluit or Rankin Inlet, or one of three liquor agents located in outer Nunavut communities. The

NLC office or liquor agent will handle your order and fax your payment. When the money has cleared, your order is shipped.

Two or three days is a long time to wait, but trust me, you'll enjoy that beer when you get it. Just don't go drinking it all at once!

 Price check: Average price in Nunavut for 24 premium domestic beer: $50, taxes included.

STEP 2: OPENING YOUR BEER

Now, in order to get the beer you just purchased down your gullet and into your belly, you are going to have to crack it open.

Generally this is a pretty simple premise. Assuming you have purchased a quantity of beer suitable for your own personal use—and I'm not talking about a magnum of Labatt Maximum Ice—you have more than likely bought cans or bottles.

The Beer Can

The aluminum beer can turned 50 years old this year on January 22, 2009. Invented by the Coors Brewing Company in 1959, the aluminum can replaced the tin can, which came in flat-top (think a can of beans) and cone-top varieties. The cone-top can was a custom-made tin can with a top that narrowed to a mouth that was then capped with a crown cap, just like a glass bottle is today.

If you have somehow found a way to live life devoid of all personal-sized carbonated beverages since 1975, the year the stay tab was introduced—or you are from Prince Edward Island—here is how you open a beer can. Find the ring on top, wedge your finger underneath the end that has not been fastened to the can and then pull up, using the ring as a lever to force open the pre-scored tab, which then folds itself into the beverage, hence the name "stay" tab. If you can't figure this out, chances are someone else has opened and served you one too many: go ahead and pass your beer to someone who can still taste it.

The Beer Bottle

If you've bought bottled beer, then you have faced the opening of five possible sealing methods.

Twist-offs

By far the most ubiquitous method used to seal beer bottles, it is hard to believe that the twist-off is only celebrating its 25th birthday. Twist-off caps were developed and introduced to the beer world by Labatt in 1984. The product innovation was in response to a secretly planned market-share coup executed by Carling O'Keefe a year earlier in 1983, when the brewer scored a major win with the introduction of the American lager Miller High Life. The move to bring "the Champagne of Beers" to Canada—dubbed Operation "Northern Elk" by Carling O'Keefe executives—was coupled with distributing it in long-neck bottles at a time when the stubby was still the industry standard. This move, which caught the innovation-starved beer consumer's attention, rocked both Molson and Labatt who were in a three-way market-share war with Carling O'Keefe. And so, Labatt, considered the brewer of innovation among the Big Three, launched the twist-off cap in its own shroud of secrecy.

Employing a smokescreen strategy, Labatt first rolled out "Project Smokey." Project Smokey became the bait for both Carling O'Keefe and Molson, as Labatt aired commercials showing Labatt Lite in tall bottles similar to the Miller bottles Carling O'Keefe had debuted in 1983. As Paul Brent says in his book *Lager Heads*, Project Smokey prompted Molson, for fear of being left behind as the only major brewer using stubbies, to join the long-neck bottle game. A few weeks later,

Labatt launched a second campaign: "Project Czar." In dramatic fashion, advertisements showed a hand effortlessly twisting off the cap of a long-neck bottle of Labatt Lite. Carling O'Keefe and Molson, already swimming in long-neck, non-twist-cap bottles, were both left with their pants down as Labatt gained a two-percent market share (valued at about $30 million).

Twist-offs are here to stay, and the caps are generally pretty easy to use: wrap your hand around the cap, twist in a counter-clockwise motion and presto! Beer! (Remember, as with most twisty things in life: counter-clockwise = twist it off; clockwise = twist it on. Or, lefty, loosey; righty, tighty). But if you plan on drinking all day, twist-offs can potentially hurt your hand after a while. The solution? Place a bar towel over the cap before you twist. The advantage? It saves your hand, plus it looks fancy. Note: you will never look fancy, no matter what you have chosen to do, if you also made the choice to wear a Labatt Wildcat T-shirt.

Crown Caps
If you didn't buy twist-offs, chances are you have purchased crown caps. Crown caps are circular pieces of metal with a rubber backing that are fastened to the bottle by being pinched under the bottom edge of the bottle's lip. William Painter and his Crown Cork & Seal Corporation patented this method of capping in 1892. Prior to Painter's invention, most bottled beers were sealed with a cork stopper, which was far less efficient than Painter's cap.

DO NOT try to twist off a crown cap. It will only lead to a world of pain, and if your friends aren't very nice, some

mild hazing. In order to get your suds out of a crown-capped bottle, tradition holds that you use a bottle opener, also known as a church key (for its shape). Fittingly, Painter invented the bottle opener as well, but, funnily enough, he didn't receive the patent for this product until two years after he received the patent for the crown cap.

As with the twist-off, opening the crown cap is a pretty simple premise: use the bottle opener as a lever with one edge of it underneath the bottom of the bottle cap and the opposite edge resting on the middle of the top of the cap. Now, pry upward and thank Mr. Painter—beer awaits.

DID YOU  KNOW?

It is possible to open a crown cap without a church key. If the congregation is rocking and you're locked out of the House of Suds, you can employ the smashy-smashy technique—a technical name that you will want to use with reverence. First, find a hard surface with an edge that is close to a 90-degree angle. Fortunately many places that you find beer also have these edges: kitchens with countertops, backyard get-togethers with decks and campsites with rocks. Second, place the bottom edge of the crown cap against the top of the edge of the hard surface you have found. Now, take your hand and smash a flat palm on the centre of the cap. The force of this hit should send the bottle down while the edge of the hard surface pries the crown cap off. Didn't work? Try it again—smashy, smashy, remember?

Screw Caps
If you purchased a bottle with a metal or plastic pop-bottle-style screw cap, chances are you have just bought yourself some pretty bad beer, or worse yet, malt liquor. If you have any self-respect, take the beer back and get yourself a real one. The obvious reason you shouldn't want to drink malt liquor is the amount of adjunct ingredients used to give the beverage its mellow-yellow complexion and its high alcohol content. Then again, maybe that is all you're after. Malt liquor tastes best when accompanied by a mustard-stained white tank top.

Swing-top Caps
This type of cap is featured most prominently by the Dutch brand Grolsch. In 1897, Theo de Groen, then-director of Grolsch, invented the swing-top cap. It used a ceramic head,

a rubber ring and a metal clamp. De Groen's creation gave beer drinkers an easy way to both open and store beer, as the pressure applied by the clamp on the rubber seal that sat around the ceramic top kept air out and CO_2 in. The swing-top cap kept beer fresh for another day of drinking.

Opening a swing-top-capped bottle is fun: grab the bottle with two hands and place it so that the arms of the metal clamp swoop toward you. Place one thumb on each of the metal arms and hold the body of the bottle with your remaining fingers. Push the arms away from you with your thumbs—pop! Beer! Yes.

Corks

You don't see many corked beers these days; oftentimes they will only appear with Lambics, special-edition winter-warmers, festival brews and Trappist ales. When encountering a corked bottle, open it like you would champagne: take the chilled bottle, remove any foil or wax and the wire cage. Next, take a bar towel and drape it over the cork. Tightly grip the towel and the cork and hold the bottle, cork-side-up, on a slight angle. With your other hand rotate the fat part of the bottle until the cork pops—yummy beer!

STEP 3: POURING YOUR BEER

You obviously want to drink the beer you just opened, but wait! Not so fast. It's not as simple as you might think.

Put it in a Glass

My friend Jay has a saying that goes, "Why dirty a clean glass when my beer comes in its own glass?" While his statement definitely has a few truths to it, and there are certainly times when you should drink from the bottle—say, while camping, at rock shows or at strip clubs—pouring your beer into a glass will allow you to appreciate your brew that much more. (If you find yourself trying to appreciate your beer during any of the three activities previously mentioned, just stop. Everything has a time and place, and those activities are times and places where beer should be guzzled, not preened over.)

When you pour your bottled beer into a glass, you release carbon dioxide that would otherwise stay in the bottle's neck. The CO_2 is what gives bottled beer its fizziness, and when beer is poured, its head. CO_2 isn't inherently bad, but you do want some of it released and the rest of it dispersed throughout your beer. What you don't want is for the gas to be the first thing in your belly. This makes you bloated and full, and we know what happens when you're bloated and full— music. Exactly.

Pouring your suds into a glass also allows you to enjoy both the colour and aroma of the beer. Trying to take note of these things when drinking big-label, mainstream brews can leave you wondering what you're looking for, but with craft brews, colour and aroma certainly enhance the drinking experience.

When choosing a glass, pick one that can hold the entire contents of the can or bottle you are pouring from. This isn't a hard-and-fast rule, but it will help you employ the proper pouring technique, which will in turn reward you with a great presentation. There is something to be said for serving a great-looking beer. Our eyes do a lot of drinking for us, and the appetizing image of a perfectly poured pint—the one with the two-finger-thick head rising just above the cusp of the glass—will help you enjoy your beer that much more.

Choosing a Glass

Beer drinkers, like the rest of the alcohol-drinking world, employ different styles of glassware for different types of beer. These various drinking instruments enhance the select styles of beer that are meant to be quaffed from them. This is not to say that if you don't have a goblet you can't drink the barley wine you just purchased, but instead, if you did have said goblet, that barley wine could go from great to perfect.

Glass varieties are numerous and often called by more than one name. To confuse things further, beer companies often release their own special glassware for their own brews. In order to simplify the already muddied waters of beer glassware, think of your options as fancy, kind of fancy or not fancy at all. (While this hierarchical labelling might irk some beer connoisseurs who are quite rightfully trying to level the beer playing field by suggesting that no one style is superior to another—because it is all a matter of opinion—it still goes without saying that if a certain type of beer is best served in a stemmed glass, then that beer is fancy, end of story.)

Fancy

Anything stemmed is fancy. The round bottoms, curved sides and narrow mouths (in proportion to the widest part of the body) of flutes, tulips, goblets and chalices help capture aromas and retain carbonation. Typically these glasses are reserved for strong ales, Belgian-style fruit beers, barley wines and other malty, high-alcohol-content brews.

Kind of Fancy

Footed glassware is kind of fancy. The most prominent of footed glassware is the flared Pilsner glass. This straight glass, narrow at the bottom and wide at the top, promotes the golden colour, effervescence and clarity that good Pilsner is known for. The wide mouth allows for a generous head. The wheat-beer glass is another popular footed glass that is generally taller than the Pilsner glass and has an hourglass figure to help promote aroma.

Not Fancy at All

Mugs and pints aren't fancy, and their utilitarian design makes them perfect for the pub. From thick dimpled mugs to sleeved pints (the sleeve is the bulge three-quarters of the way up the glass that protects the rim in the case of a knock-over), any beer can be served in these glasses. However, they really excel with ales, lagers, porters and stouts, as the wide mouth affords ample room for a good head and the thick glass can stand up to many toasts and roasts.

Glass Care

If you go through all the trouble of researching and purchasing a nice beer glass, then you might as well care for it, too. Glass care is pretty simple. Just like you wouldn't use vinegar in the coffee pot (you don't, right?), you need to be careful with what you use to wash your glass. Soap can leave behind oils that emulsify with beer and break down the head, or worse, contribute to the distortion of the beer's flavour. The same goes for grease from food and your skin. The solution? Wash your beer glass in hot water with baking soda; use a bristle brush, not a cloth, and let the glass air-dry.

Pour it Over

Now that you've got a glass and it's clean, it's time to pour something into it. There are a few tricks to pouring different styles of beer, and these tricks will allow you to get the suds from its packaging to the glass—properly.

Pouring Craft Ales and Lagers
For most craft beers, it is best to start the pour with a straight drop, right down the centre of the glass to its bottom. This pouring style helps release the gas from the packaging and gives your beer a nice head. Once that lovely, rich head has formed (something that happens very quickly), tilt the glass and continue to slowly empty the rest of the contents down the side of the glass. As the vessel from which you are pouring becomes increasingly empty, slowly tilt the glass back to its upright position and add the last drops from the bottle or can. If you have to stop a few times during the pour to let the beer's head settle a little, that's okay. As you work on your technique, this will happen less and less.

Pouring Wheat Beers
This style of beer is known for its high carbonation, which results in a rich, foamy and often large head. Wheat beer needs a little more care in its pour. No drop-shots here. A good tip is to rinse the inside of your glass with cold water before you start to pour. Wetting the glass helps control the head buildup. Take your time pouring this style of beer. Be

gentle. Otherwise you could end up with all head and no body; that reminds me of a joke....

Pouring North American Lagers

Ah, the straw-coloured beers made by the big guys, Molson, Labatt, Bud, among others. The beer that typically comes from these brewers is very carbonated and relatively thin in body. Slowly pour these North American lagers down the side of your glass, but don't employ the drop-shot, as the head on these beers can quickly get out of control. If by accident you are a little cavalier with your pour, don't worry. The head you just made will dissipate quickly. Next time, just be patient and pour these beers slowly.

Pouring Bottle-conditioned Beers

These unfiltered beers have yeast sediment (also known as the dregs) at the bottom of their bottles. Do not shake the bottle to reintroduce the yeast to the body of the beer. Instead, bottle-conditioned beers should be poured slowly, with a good tilt on the glass, which helps control the amount of beer going into the glass and keeps the sediment at the bottom of the bottle. Most often you want to leave the dregs of the beer in the bottle. However, there is nothing wrong with drinking the yeast sediment. In fact, some brewers insist that you do, but if you drink the dregs, the mouth feel and taste of the beer will change, as the yeast can be gritty and bitter. Read the label of the bottle-conditioned beer you are pouring, as many come with specific directions.

Pouring Nitrogen-infused Beers

Certain brewers, like Guinness, don't use carbon dioxide to make their beers bubbly; instead, they are infused with nitrogen gas. This switch translates into a beer that is much more densely packed and whose mouth feel is thicker, richer and smoother. The head of a nitrogen-infused beer is quite velvety. In 1988, Guinness introduced the widget: a contraption placed inside the beer can or bottle that holds nitrogen. Upon a pressure change (i.e., opening the can or bottle), the widget releases nitrogen throughout the body of the beer. With nitrogen-infused beer, you must have a glass that will accommodate the entire can or bottle.

Pouring this type of beer should not be a delicate affair: open the bottle or can and dump it on in. All of it! It will take a moment to settle, but the jarring action of dumping the beer is integral to the finish of this packaged brew.

STEP 4: TASTING YOUR BEER

Generally you are going to open your beer (of course), pour it in a glass (hopefully), take a brief moment to reflect (maybe?) and then down she goes (definitely). This whole process is fine for your second, third, fourth, fifth and sixth beers of the night, but with your first beer, especially if you are drinking something a little more special than the buck-a-beer lager you found in the fridge, you might want to employ the five steps of beer tasting.

Step 1: Use Your Eyes

Don't just see your beer—*look* at your beer. Drinking happens with all the senses, so take some time to look at that freshly poured glass of beer. Beautiful, isn't it?

Notice the colour of the beer; different styles of beer can vary tremendously in colour, but this is not to say that a certain colour is indicative of a certain taste. For example, a lager like Waterloo Dark, brewed in Ontario by the Brick Brewing Company, is as black as cola, but is thin and light with a malty, sweet start and a lightly hopped finish—not at all what you expect from a first glance.

Take note of the clarity of the brew; clarity is important to some styles, like Pilsner (whose trademark is a crisp, golden appearance), while a cloudy drink can also be the sign of a good wheat beer. If a beer isn't clear, that's okay. Many beers aren't made to be clear, and as beer judge Marty Nachel points out, clarity is often the result of modern brewing techniques— in which brewers filter the beer to remove excess yeast—and nothing more. If you need to drink a clear beer, stick with the

Molsons and Labatts of the world. Otherwise, enjoy all the different clarities the beer universe has to offer.

Another thing to look for: the size of the head. A good head can tell you a lot about the quality of a beer, or the cleanliness of the glass you're drinking from. If a beer can't maintain a head, the beer may be flat, or the glass may have residual oils from its last use that have contributed to the head breaking down. A healthy head should be about two fingers thick, or close to one inch, with bubbles that are tiny. Ideally, beer should maintain some head down to the last sip.

Step 2: The Swirl

Swirl your beer gently. This will release the important aromatic properties of the beer. Be careful, though. As beer expert Michael Jackson notes, swirling in public has a tendency to look pretentious.

Step 3: Use Your Sniffer

Sniff away. If you don't want to swirl for fear of rolling eyes, you can instead do some sniffing when you first pour your beer and the aromatics of it are released. Depending on the malts and hops used, you might smell a wide variety of things, from chocolate to citrus to pine needles. Smelling is a vital step of beer tasting, as much of what we taste comes from our sense of smell.

Step 4: Time to Taste

Sip. This isn't a chugging contest, so take a small, manageable sip that you are able to track as it cascades from the tip to the back of your tongue. Beer has distinct flavours that present themselves at the tip, middle and back of the tongue. Because of these flavours, don't swallow your sip right away. Instead, swirl it around in your mouth once before swallowing in order to get a well-rounded profile of the beer's overall taste. Swirling marries the flavours experienced at the tip and middle of the tongue. Upon swallowing, the back of your tongue experiences the finish, which is often slightly more bitter than the tastes experienced at the middle and the tip. The finish is followed shortly by the aftertaste. This entire trip, from tip to aftertaste, forms the taste profile of a beer, and it is often complex. As a result, it is important to note how the beer tasted at all different regions and points of the sip.

While you taste the beer as it swishes around in your mouth, also pay attention to its consistency, which is articulated by a description called "mouth feel" (as referenced a few times in this chapter). Mouth feel is an important factor in tasting as it helps identify whether the beer has done a good job in representing the family it belongs to. The mouth feel, like the other beer-tasting steps, is a key component in the overall enjoyment of your brew.

Step 5: Make Some Notes

The unofficial fifth step of beer tasting is to reflect on steps one through four. Often we are too consumed with what is going on around us to truly appreciate what it is that we are ingesting. A brief moment to collect your thoughts on what you just tasted will do wonders for your beer appreciation and evaluation of future pints.

Following these steps allows you to fully experience your beer and enhance your enjoyment of it. If having multiple, different beers in an evening, conduct steps one to four (and maybe five) with each brew, making sure to drink water or eat plain bread in between samples in order to cleanse the palate. Avoid greasy or salty foods: they distort the taste of beer.

One Particular Note for Those Set on Tasting Beer

People often try to fit beer made in Canada and the United States into already established styles from other parts of the world. It should be noted that although many North American brews are of an international style, and should be viewed accordingly, some are members of a particular North American style (like cream ale) and are not necessarily subject to the same style guidelines delineated for foreign beer. As well, the international styles of beer we produce often use local varieties of barley and hops, which will have different flavour profiles than their international counterparts. As such, Canadian and American beer should not be penalized for this seeming departure from international style, but instead celebrated for their unique addition to the world of beer. Beware of anyone critiquing beer who routinely views North American brew as inferior to foreign beer due these differences. An educated beer drinker will acknowledge that some Canadian and American beers possess a distinct North American taste, others very nicely capture the flavours and essence of an international style, while still others represent a wholly unique North American style.

STEP 5: STORING YOUR BEER

You can't drink more than one beer at a time. Well, you *can,* but it involves much more than a beer and a beer glass, and it is quite often coupled with a fraternity. So unless you are funnelling an entire six-pack, you'll need to store your beer somewhere.

Where to Put It

The refrigerator is the obvious choice for storing most perishable items, and the majority of North American–style beers are no different. The temperature in the fridge (around 5°C) is great for storing lagers, Pilsners, wheat beers and even light ales, but you'll want to serve them closer to 6°C or 7°C. Cellar temperatures (around 12°C) are suitable for standard ales, stouts, porters, Lambics and bitters. Storage areas that hover just below room temperature (around 15°C) are best for high-alcohol-content brews like dark ales and barley wines. A good guideline to follow is that the lower the alcohol content, the colder optimal storage conditions should be. If you store all of your beer in the fridge, that's okay—just try to serve each particular brew as if it had come from the right storage temperature. Beer that is served too cold will lose a lot of its taste and aroma, something you don't want to deprive yourself of. That is, unless you're chugging a can after playing hockey. In this case, make it as cold as possible, please.

Beer Kryptonite

Beer has three big enemies: light, heat and time. All have the ability to ruin a perfectly good brew. Excessive heat and long shelf times increase the natural oxidation of beer and render it stale. Light, on the other hand, turns a beer skunky. If you have ever encountered a skunky beer you know exactly how it smells, but this description is more than just a clever term. It has been scientifically proven that the alpha acids produced by boiling the hops in the brewing process react in the finished beer when hit with visible or ultraviolet light. This reaction creates free radicals that react with proteins in the beer containing sulphur, and together they create a chemical compound that is almost identical to the compound produced by skunks. So, basically, you wouldn't lick a skunk, so don't drink a skunky beer. Send it back or pour it down the drain.

To avoid having skunky or stale beer, it is important that your cold storage also be dark storage. Many brewers choose to package their beer in brown or amber glass as a method of conservation, but these bottles aren't perfect. Even worse, clear and green glass bottles, popular for showcasing the colour and clarity of beer, do nothing to protect the brew from light. As such, take extra care with beer packaged this way. As a general rule, beer + light = bad, and beer + heat = bad.

STEP 6: RETURNING YOUR EMPTIES

The Bottle-return Story

The bottle-return system in Canada is one of international envy. It is a model many countries look to emulate, and it helps divert over one million tonnes of waste from Canadian landfills. But the system didn't used to work that way. The Canadian brewing industry operated under a model like most other brewing industries across the globe: a system focused on the production and sale of beer and not much else. In 1942, brewers, distillers and wineries cross-country were forced to reduce outputs because of the Wartime Alcoholic Beverages Order. With everything from barley to wood being rationed for the war effort, brewers had no choice but to retool their operations. The most significant change in operations was a conservation strategy developed to replace the wooden crates consumers were using to transport and store their beer. As the war effort ramped up, Canadian brewers rolled out a reusable corrugated cardboard box that replaced the need for wooden crates. This was the first initiative of its kind in the brewing sector. Shortly after the change brought about by the Beverages Order, the Brewers Association of Canada was formed in 1943. This organization was eventually an industry leader in environmental innovation, but it took some time for the association to get where it is today.

The beer industry didn't think again about consumable-packaging products until the 1962 introduction of the first Industry Standard Bottle, the stubby. The stubby was a money-saving effort spearheaded by the Brewers Association of Canada, first and foremost, but along with saving dollars, the initiative also helped Canadian brewers divert waste, and lots of it. You only

have to look at the innovations the stubby provided the industry to understand how greatly it changed the constitution of Canadian landfills. Previous to the stubby, returning beer bottles to the brewer was not an efficient task, and the majority of bottles simply ended up in the trash. With the introduction of the closed-loop bottle-return system, consumers could return their stubbies and be certain that any bottle brought back was a bottle diverted from a landfill. Even bottles that were deemed unusable were smashed, re-melted and turned into glass for new bottles. The stubby was also an efficient size to pack. With its small size, a case of stubbies used less cardboard than its ancestors did and could be stored more compactly in haulers and warehouses, creating more efficient shipments and space usage.

The stubby was a utilitarian product: it was practical, saved brewers money and kept Canada cleaner. But like many products whose main purpose is functionality, the stubby lacked sex appeal. In the end, the Canadian brewing industry curbed the stubby for something less efficient but more desirable. The culprit? Long-neck, non-returnable, non-refillable bottles (also known as private-mould bottles).

The private-mould era lasted from 1984 to 1993, after which the brewing industry reverted back to the closed-loop Industry Standard Bottle system—the same system still in place today.

In 2005, the Brewers Association of Canada reported that of Canada's total beer sales, 66 percent were in bottles, while cans made up 24 percent and draught made up the final 10 percent. Regionally, every province but Alberta and BC prefer bottles to cans, with 55 percent of total beer sales in Alberta and 58 percent of total sales in BC coming from the purchase of the can. The return numbers on beer bottles and cans across Canada are staggeringly high, with 97 percent of bottles and 82 percent of cans delivered back into the system by consumers. Counting bottles alone, the numbers represent 1.3 million tonnes of waste diverted from landfills and the reduction of 187,000 tonnes of greenhouse gas emissions from the would-be manufacturing and processing of new bottles. Not all bottles returned are Industry Standard Bottles, though. In Ontario, 23 percent of all beer bottles returned were non-refillable bottles. But non-refillables are still recycled and in many instances turned into new bottles or reused for other applications, such as fibreglass.

The Brewers Association of Canada also reclaims all the packaging it creates. Kegs last up to 50 years and after a life cycle are crushed and recycled. In addition, cardboard boxes are crushed and recycled, while beer caps are melted down and reused. Even forklift pallets and other industrial waste are recaptured.

The Industry Standard Bottle closed-loop system, however, isn't perfectly green. The system does need water and cleaning chemicals, plus it has to ship its product in order to reuse its bottles. Just how much water, chemicals, emissions and waste is created from the closed-loop system is uncertain, as there is no uniform agency that provides the service, and many brewers take on the cleaning process themselves.

For you, though, it is about returning your empties—and more. Collect all empty beer containers, no matter the makeup, and also keep beer caps and boxes; everything can and should be returned. We are sometimes not the most responsible people when we have had one too many, so let's make sure to be responsible when cleaning up the mess.

Here is how to return your empties…

BC

In the tree-hugger capital of Canada, you'd think that returning bottles for a refund would be simple—and it is, but only kind of. Encorp Pacific, a federally incorporated, not-for-profit corporation, handles the majority of BC's beverage-container management through Return-it Depot centres. Consumers can return almost any bottle, from any previous purpose, receive the appropriate refund and have that bottle recycled properly. The only two items Return-it Depots don't fully refund are Industry Standard Bottles and aluminum beer cans—instead, some of the refund is kept as a handling fee.

At BC Liquor Stores, rural outlets and licensee stores, consumers receive a full refund on any beverage-alcohol container purchased in the province—but there is a catch. While you can drop off your Industry Standard Bottles and aluminum cans, you can only do so in quantities of no more than 24 per day.

Alberta

It isn't often in Alberta you'll find a liquor retailer that also accepts bottle returns. While all liquor vendors in the province *can* accept bottle returns, they don't *have* to accept them. If you are stuck with an unwilling retailer, or simply can't find a retailer that accepts empties, you can drop your containers off for a 10-cent refund at any of the 216 registered bottle depots in the province. These depots are privately run businesses that work with the Beverage Container Management Board (BCMB), a conglomeration of public and private enterprises and environmental groups responsible for all recycling in Alberta. While beer consumers receive a full deposit refund when visiting any bottle depot, the BCMB also charges (at initial purchase) a container-recycling fee (CRF). Currently, there is no CRF fee for aluminum cans or Industry Standard Bottles, but non-refillable glass beer bottles, mostly used by specialty brands and imports, have a five-cent CRF fee attached to every bottle, making your initial investment 15 cents per bottle as opposed to the standard 10-cent deposit fee.

Bottle depots in Alberta also accept all refundable containers including box wine, Tetra Paks and, since June 1, 2009, specially marked milk containers.

Saskatchewan

Saskatchewan has one of the most unique bottle-deposit systems in all of North America. Although Industry Standard Bottles can be returned for refund at any SLGA Liquor Store or franchise location, bottles and cans of all kinds can be returned for refund at any of the province's 70 SARCAN bottle depots.

SARCAN is the 21-year-old bottle-recycling program initiated by Saskatchewan in 1988 as an arm of the Saskatchewan Association of Rehabilitation Centres, or SARC. With this program, Saskatchewan launched one of the most successful affirmative employment opportunities in Canada for individuals with disabilities. SARCAN's workforce is full of people of all abilities, with a large share of jobs belonging to people with disabilities. All of SARCAN's employees receive competitive wages, benefits and a pension.

When Saskatchewanian consumers purchase bottled beverages (aside from beer packaged in the Industry Standard Bottle), an environmental levy is charged along with a deposit fee. Usually close to five cents, the environmental levy helps pay for depot service in the province. Refillable 341-millilitre beer-bottle deposits average 10 cents across Canada, but in Saskatchewan the deposit is only four cents, and the full amount is always refunded to the consumer.

Manitoba

When it comes to packaging in Manitoba, if you purchased beer in it, it's returnable. Beer containers have the honour of being the only reclaimed packaging by the beverage-alcohol industry in Manitoba; spirit and wine containers are still collected with the province's blue-box program.

To return your empty bottles and cans, you need to go to the nearest beer vendor. The MLCC provides compensation to beer vendors for handling empties but does not reclaim any beverage containers itself.

Ontario

Ontario just might be the greatest place in Canada for beverage-alcohol recycling. For all its faults and negative press, one thing is certain about The Beer Store: its system for recapturing beverage-alcohol waste is bar none. For as

long as there has been an Industry Standard Bottle, The Beer Store has accepted beer-bottle returns, but in 2007, The Beer Store entered into a five-year agreement with the Ontario government to not only accept the return of beer bottles, but also any other beverage-alcohol container— even box wine! With this initiative, Ontarians can return all bottles, tetra packs, cans and bag-in-box items to The Beer Store for a full refund. The Beer Store accepts all packaging, bottle caps, six-pack plastic rings and plastic bags as well.

If you are returning more than 120 bottles at a time or running a bottle drive, The Beer Store encourages you to go to one of its 215 locations that handle bulk returns.

Québec

Taking your empty beer containers back to where you first purchased them is pretty standard when it comes to La Belle Province. The SAQ accepts returns, but only on the bottled products they sell—liquor, wine and imported beer. Industry Standard Bottles and anything else used by domestic brewers can usually be returned for a full refund to the grocery or convenience store they were purchased from. Some stores don't allow for the return of empties because of space restrictions, but, with so much competition in the domestic beer market, many stores take back empties simply because they want you to come back.

Newfoundland

Recycling initiatives in Newfoundland and Labrador are the domain of the Multi-Materials Stewardship Board (MMSB). Part of the MMSB mandate is to strategically grow its privately run Green Depot network that handles used beverage containers. Currently, the province has 63 locations where citizens can return used beverage containers, including beer bottles, for a full refund.

Convenience stores that sell beer are also allowed to accept beer empties for refund, provided they are not non-refillable bottles.

Nova Scotia

When it comes time to return empties in Nova Scotia, there are 83 private-industry bottle depots, locally known as Enviro-Depots, that meet the needs of beer consumers across the province. These bottle-return stations operate as part of a wider waste-reduction system in Nova Scotia called the Resource Recovery Fund Board Inc., or RRFB Nova Scotia. This non-profit organization, which works with both the government and private industry, handles all consumer waste management in the province.

Enviro-Depots, contracted out by the RRFB, collect all types of beer containers, but consumers are only refunded half of their initial bottle deposit. So if a beer bottle had a deposit of 10 cents, you will only receive five cents in return. The remaining money on the deposit goes to the Enviro-Depot, as does a sorting fee paid to the depot by the RRFB.

New Brunswick

In New Brunswick, the Department of the Environment directly oversees the recycling of all containers in the province, including the return of beer bottles. Bottles and cans can be returned to any of the 79 sanctioned redemption centres in the province. Redemption centres are private businesses whose main source of income is derived from collecting a share of the bottle-deposit refund.

For Industry Standard Bottles, beer consumers receive a full refund, while non-refillable bottles and cans garner a refund of half the initial deposit.

Prince Edward Island

As touched on, Prince Edward Island used to have a pretty unique beverage-container system in place, as the province, after banning canned beer in 1973 and canned pop in 1984, was the only place in North America where consumers could not purchase carbonated beverages in cans. The "can ban" was put in place to protect PEI jobs and the environment. With the ban, and a similar ban on plastic non-refillable containers of pop, the entire province worked on a refillable glass-bottle standard.

All that changed in May 2008 when legislation came into effect that introduced carbonated canned beverages back into the system.

Islanders used to return their empties at the PEILCC and get a deposit back on Industry Standard Bottles. Not anymore. PEI has now implemented a depot-based beverage-container management system that is modelled after the rest of the Maritime provinces.

Consumers in PEI who want to collect a refund on beverage containers, including beer, need to go to one of the 10 Container Recycling Depots across the province. Much the way this system works in other provinces, consumers in PEI are only given half of the allotted refund, while the other half is collected for depot and handling fees.

Northwest Territories

If you want to return bottles in the Northwest Territories, you will have to do it through the Beverage Container Program, initiated by the territory in 2005. Under the program, all bottles can be returned to bottle depots for refund. Twenty-four permanent depots currently operate in the Northwest Territories, all of which are privately run businesses. In peak times, another six temporary depots are opened to collect beverage containers in communities that don't have their own depot and are considered too far from the closest neighbouring depot.

Under the Beverage Container Program, beverage containers have an additional handling fee built into their price, on top of the deposit. The majority of beer bottles are levied with an additional 10-cent fee, while most beer cans have an additional five-cent charge. The handling fee covers depot and distribution costs.

Yukon

The Beverage Container Recycling Program allows residents of the Yukon to return beverage containers for refund to any one of the 24 affiliated depots across the territory. Like many other depot-based recycling programs, private-enterprise depots are sanctioned to collect beverage containers on the territory's behalf. To help finance the system, the Yukon government administers a recycling fee that is incorporated into the price of goods that are sold in recyclable beverage containers. Consumers purchasing beer issued in the Industry Standard Bottle do not have to pay a recycling fee, because the bottle is reused. Returning these bottles garners a full refund.

Nunavut

There isn't much choice when it comes to returning bottles and cans in the 10-year-old territory of Nunavut. But to its credit, Nunavut has established two bottle depots, one in Iqaluit and one in Rankin Inlet. At either location, residents can return any beverage container, except milk, for a refund of five cents. Beverage containers are condensed, baled and sent on barges to southern communities where they can be processed.

FOOD PAIRINGS

Food and drink pairing, something that was almost exclusively the domain of wine, has become popular in beer circles. No longer is it the general rule that beer is reserved for quaffing while barbecuing. Today, many restaurants are dedicated solely to the practice of pairing beer with their food. Although having a beer while standing at the barbecue is still a great pastime, you should also start thinking about which beer you are going to pair with that steak you are flipping.

Cut, Contrast, Complement

These three simple words will point you in the right direction when you are pairing beer and food. The hardest thing to conquer when pairing is the delicate balance of the dish complementing the beverage and vice versa. Attempt with your pairings to exploit the differences or enhance the similarities in your food and beer choices. For instance, hops do well in cutting grease and vinegar; malts balance tart, bitter foods. On the most elementary of levels, you can look at beer pairing in the same light as wine pairing—lighter foods often go with light-coloured beer, while darker foods usually go with dark-coloured beer. But don't be afraid to mix it up. Rich, heavy foods tend to work well with dark, robust beers but can be equally as enjoyable with a crisp, clean offering.

German Food, German Beer?

Different cultures and ethnicities have developed certain gastronomic profiles for a reason—they used what was available to them to create dishes and pairings that worked. Germans eating a heavy schnitzel dinner are, of course, well-aided by

the clean, crisp, cutting qualities of a German Pilsner. The British, on the other hand, do well marrying a steak and kidney pie with a pale ale or a bitter. Think globally when preparing your pairings, and don't be afraid to mix cultures; maybe a German wheat beer is exactly what that spicy Jamaican dish needs!

When in doubt, keep it simple and remember there are no set rules. Even at its worst, a failed pairing won't be that bad. I mean, you are already *eating* and *drinking*, which, to me, sounds like a pretty great pairing in itself!

For the Faint of Palate

If you don't feel like experimenting—or trusting your senses— here are some classic combinations that win every time.

- **Beer and Appetizers**: Lambics (Belgian wild-yeast fermented brews) work well with appetizers because these generally zesty ales contain a broad range of flavours, including sherry-like notes, which make Lambics akin to more common aperitifs like fortified wine and champagne.

- **Beer and Salad**: Nice, leafy-green salads are complemented well by North American nut-brown ales. The nuttiness in the ale brings out the rustic characters of the salad, especially if it is made with artichokes or dandelion greens, or includes nuts such as pine nuts, walnuts and pecans.

- **Beer and Cheese**: Cheese goes well with strong ales and Belgian Trappist- or Abbey-style ales. These beers have the fortitude of alcohol and flavour to cut through the most robust of cheeses.

- **Beer and Shellfish**: Traditionally, the English pair shellfish with robust stouts and porters. Marston's of England even has a stout they call Oyster Stout. Marston's stout does not contain oysters, but some brewers have been known to include them in the brewing process.

- **Beer and Fish**: Like white wine, golden Pilsners and North American premium lagers pair well with fish. The lighter the fish, the lighter the lager should be. Save darker North American lagers and hoppy Pilsners for tuna and other heavier varieties of fish. Smoked fish is great paired with English brown ales.

- **Beer and Chicken**: When chicken is poached or grilled, a wheat beer's mellow character is called for. Roasted chicken calls for an Oktoberfest offering, whose amber body and spicy notes will hold up to the heavier flavours of the roast. When eating barbecued chicken, a North American golden ale, with its light hop profile and crisp finish, will do the trick.

- **Beer and Game Birds/Turkey**: A robust beer is needed to cut through the intense flavours of game birds. Try a North American dark or brown ale with this dish. The appropriate robust profile of these ales, with their notes of nut and sometimes coffee, will stand up to the game and complement its flavours. For lighter-tasting game try a golden ale.

- **Beer and Pork**: The malt flavours and caramel notes of an amber ale or Irish red ale, along with their mild hop profiles, will marry well with the succulent sweetness of pork. A cream ale, whose taste is less malty, slightly more hopped than amber or Irish ale, but still soft and smooth, will contrast nicely with pork but won't overpower it.

- **Beer and Lamb**: A big-bodied beer is needed to stand up to the game-like, grassy taste of lamb. Belgian ales, with their high alcohol content, notes of fruit and spice and dry finish, help offset lamb's intense flavours. In a pinch, an India pale ale with a hop profile that is not too intense will do the trick.

- **Beer and Beef**: Golden to copper-coloured pale ales carry the perfect balance of crisp, carbonated, floral/hoppy flavours to contrast against the deep, rich taste of beef dishes. These pale ales, with their light malt profile, work well in this instance, while India pale ales and golden ales can also stand in when pairing beer with beef.

- **Beer and Pizza/Burgers and other Barbecued Sandwiches**: North American premium lager and North American red lager are perfect with these bready offerings. The carbonation, low malt profile and crisp flavours of the lager cut through the bread and don't overpower the meat and other toppings.

DID YOU  KNOW?

If you are having a beer-paired dinner party, it is okay not to serve everyone an entire bottle of beer with every pairing. This is especially true if you are serving more than three courses. The point of beer pairing is to experience the different flavour combinations that are created between various beers and foods. Serve an excess of beer and your guests will be too full to enjoy your mastery. Stick to beer servings of about six to eight ounces, and if your guests are up for it, polish off the remaining brew after the last course of your meal.

COOKING WITH BEER

Cooking with beer is great. It lets you employ the "one for me, one for you" system. Aside from that, it also allows you to play with a wide world of flavours that other alcohols can't match.

The Lowdown

Beer is a liquid that doesn't often have a high ABV rate. Thus, in cooking (not baking), you can basically substitute beer in the place of water in almost any recipe. With this easy method of culinary experimentation, keep in mind that the beer chosen in your food-beer pairings will most often also cook well with that same food.

Recipes

Stout Reduction

Reductions and gravies are great ways to add beer to a meal without too much labour. Sauces allow you to create a base or an accent for your meal, and they are easily adaptable for many applications and palates.

Savoury Version

2 cups stout (such as McAuslan's Oatmeal Stout)

1 Tbsp sugar

½ tsp salt

½ Tbsp butter (optional)

Mix the stout, sugar and salt in a pot; bring mixture to a boil. Boil until the stout reaches the consistency of maple syrup— a cooking time of approximately 11 minutes. Cool mixture for 5 minutes (it will thicken more as it cools), then mix in the butter, if desired (this will yield a richer sauce).

Sweet Version

Use the same ingredients as above, but omit the salt and add an extra 1 Tbsp of sugar. Use the same cooking process as the Savoury Version.

Recipe will yield ¼ cup of the reduction.

How to use: The savoury reduction works well with steak, beef, ribs, lamb shanks and other cuts of red meat, as well as with vegetables such as mushrooms and asparagus. It also goes well with mussels and other shellfish.

Use the sweet reduction as a simple syrup for desserts. Serve drizzled on fruit or with cake, brownies, crepes or waffles.

Chunky Beer Gravy

350 g ground beef/turkey/veggie ground round (soy protein)
1–2 Tbsp oil (vegetable or olive)
2 Tbsp all-purpose flour
1 Tbsp sugar
1½ cup amber ale (such as the Phillips Brewing Company's Blue Buck)
1 cup water
2 tsp Dijon mustard
salt and pepper, to taste

Sauté the beef/turkey or soy protein in a deep pan or pot in the oil until well browned. Sprinkle in the flour and sugar, mix well. Add and mix in the amber ale, water and mustard. Bring the gravy to a boil, season with salt and pepper, and thicken to desired consistency.

How to use: Serve the gravy on French fries, hot dogs, sausages or alone on bread as a "manwich." You can also add it to fresh-cut fries and smoked cheddar for an unbelievable poutine. The gravy also works well with minced green onion, cheese, sour cream and salsa on nachos or as a well-thickened portion with eggs and toast.

Tip: For a thinner gravy, add more ale.

 Next time you make a roast, try making the gravy with beer instead of water.

Potato Chambly Soup

2 leeks, washed and sliced

2–3 Tbsp butter or olive oil

5 potatoes (starchy, like russets), peeled and cut into 1-inch
pieces

4 cups Blanche de Chambly (or another Belgian-style wheat
beer)

4 cups water or light stock (vegetable works well)

salt and pepper, to taste

½ cup heavy cream (optional)

Sauté the leeks, until tender, in a pot with the butter or oil.
Add the potatoes and cover with the beer and half the water
or stock. Season with a dash of salt and pepper. Simmer the
potatoes and leeks until potatoes are tender. Purée the soup
using as much of the remaining water or stock as necessary
to reach desired consistency (more beer can be substituted
for the remaining water or stock for a bigger beer flavour).
Adjust seasoning with salt and pepper. Add the heavy
cream, if desired.

How to serve: A 12–16 oz bowl will do. Serve with buttered
crusty bread. Pair the soup with the same wheat beer you used
in the recipe. If you used the heavy cream and want a beer to
cut through the creamy consistency of the soup, pair it with
a golden ale, like Vancouver Island Brewery's Piper's Pale Ale.

Beer-steamed Fish

1½ cup lager or golden ale (such as the Pump House
Brewery's Cadian Ale)

1 lime, halved

6–8 sprigs of cilantro

1–2 fillets of white fish (tilapia), 4 oz each

salt and pepper, to taste

Place the beer, one half of the lime (cut in wedges) and half of the cilantro into a pot and bring to a boil. Season each side of the fish fillet with salt and pepper and place on a steam rack in the pot. Steam the fish for approximately 6 minutes (or until the fish is opaque and flaky). Remove the fish, squeeze the juice from the remaining lime over top and sprinkle the remaining cilantro (roughly chopped) onto the fish.

How to serve: Serve the fish with seasonal, local, roasted vegetables. Pair the meal with the ale you cooked it with, or with a German-style Pilsner, such as Steam Whistle Brewing's Steam Whistle Pilsner.

Tip: The steaming liquid can also be used as a sauce.

The Ultimate Hangover Cure

The Best Pancakes are made with Canadian Beer

1½ cups all-purpose flour
¼ cup sugar
1 tsp baking powder
½ tsp salt
1 cup red ale (such as Cameron's Auburn Ale)
¼ cup milk (or substitute the milk with ale for more beer flavour)
1 large egg

In a large bowl, mix dry ingredients together. Slowly fold in ale, milk and egg. Cook pancakes in an oiled pan on a low heat, giving the centre of the pancake enough time to cook thoroughly without burning the exterior.

How to serve: Top pancakes with maple syrup and butter. Pair meal with the same beer you cooked it with—if you're hungover, sometimes the hair of the dog is better than anything else!

BEER COCKTAILS AND MOCKTAILS

Every once in a while you want a beer-plus.

Black and Tan

10 oz pale ale
10 oz stout
20-oz pint glass

Method: Pour pale ale in the pint glass. Next, take a spoon and bend the head backward—yes, ruin the spoon—so it's at a 90-degree angle with the handle. Place the spoon in the pint glass with the pale ale, keeping the spoon above the pale ale and the handle against the side of the glass (the spoon should be bent backward enough so that the convex side of the spoon faces up). Slowly pour the stout over the convex part of the spoon. This method should create a "floating" appearance, which is a result of the different densities of the two liquids.

Half and Half

10 oz lager
10 oz stout
20-oz pint glass

Method: Pour lager in the pint glass. Next, take a spoon and bend the head backward (as outlined earlier). Place the spoon in the pint glass with the lager, keeping the spoon above the lager and the handle against the side of the glass. Slowly pour the stout over the convex part of the spoon. This method should create a "floating" appearance, which is a result of the different densities of the liquids.

Black Velvet

3 oz champagne or sparkling wine
3 oz stout
7-oz champagne flute

Method: Pour champagne in the flute. Next, take a spoon and bend the head backward. Take the spoon and place it in the champagne flute, keeping the spoon above the champagne and the handle against the side of the glass. Slowly pour the stout over the convex part of the spoon. This method should create a "floating" appearance, which is a result of the different densities of the liquids.

Poor Man's Black Velvet

10 oz cider
10 oz stout
20-oz pint glass

Method: Pour cider in the pint glass. Next, take a spoon and bend the head backward. Slowly pour the stout over the convex part of the spoon. This method should create a "floating" appearance, which is the result of the different densities of the liquids.

Boilermaker

1 oz whiskey
16 oz ale
1-oz shot glass
20-oz pint glass

Method: Pour the whiskey in the shot glass. Pour the ale into the pint glass. Take the shot glass of whiskey and drop it into the pint glass of ale. Chug.

Car Bomb

½ oz Irish cream
½ oz Irish whiskey
16 oz stout
1-oz shot glass
20-oz pint glass

Method: Pour the Irish cream in the shot glass. Pour the Irish whiskey on top of the Irish cream. Pour the stout into the pint glass. Take the shot glass and drop it into the pint glass of stout. Drink fast—the cream will curdle if the drink sits too long.

Dr. Pepper

1 oz amaretto
16 oz lager
1-oz shot glass
20-oz pint glass

Method: Pour the amaretto in the shot glass. Pour the lager into the pint glass. Take the shot glass of amaretto and drop it into the pint glass of lager. Chug.

Honky Sunrise

Invented by the fine folks at Collision in Toronto, this is the perfect "breakfast beer." It is also great on hot summer days.

16 oz Blanche de Chambly (or similar Belgian-style wheat beer, or a light-tasting golden ale or lager)
2 oz orange juice
splash of cranberry juice
20-oz pint glass

Method: Pour Blanche de Chambly in the pint glass, top with orange juice and add splash of cranberry juice (to taste).

Michelada

7 oz crushed ice
1 oz tequila
dash of soy sauce
dash of Tabasco sauce
dash of Worcestershire sauce
pinch of salt and pepper
1 can of lager (12 oz)
20-oz pint glass

Method: Add ice, tequila, soy sauce, Tabasco sauce, Worcestershire sauce, salt and pepper to the pint glass and then pour lager into the glass.

Red Eye

18 oz lager
2 oz tomato juice
20-oz pint glass

Method: Pour lager into glass, top with tomato juice. Stir.

Shandy (or Shandy Gaff)

10 oz lager
10 oz ginger beer, ginger ale or lemonade
20-oz pint glass

Method: Pour lager into the pint glass, top off with ginger beer, ginger ale or lemonade. Stir.

Snakebite

10 oz lager
10 oz cider
20-oz pint glass

Method: Pour lager into the pint glass, top off with cider. Stir.

Skip and Go Naked

40 oz lager
7 oz gin (or vodka or tequila)
10 oz lemon juice
splash of grenadine
a few ice cubes
60-oz pitcher

Method: Pour lager into the pitcher. Add gin, lemon juice and grenadine. Add ice cubes to chill. Stir.

SPORTS AND BEER: THE OLDEST PASTIME THERE IS

The Guelph Maple Leafs

Canada has never been a baseball juggernaut, like, say, the U.S., but the boys north of the 44th can bring the heat with the best of them. Just ask son of brewer John Sleeman, George Sleeman, who in 1863 joined the Guelph Maple Leafs baseball club as a 22-year-old rookie pitcher. With Sleeman's help, the

Maple Leafs consistently improved between 1863 and 1869, and in 1869 won their first-ever Canadian Championship.

By 1874, Sleeman was president of the team, at which point he enlisted a few Americans to come and play for the Maple Leafs. As Sleeman was the main financial contributor to the club, he offered the American players a cut of the end-of-season profits if they came to Canada to play. Still considered an amateur club, the Maple Leafs entered and won "the non-professional championship of the world" of 1874 in Watertown, New York. By 1876, Sleeman was paying all Maple Leafs players money (not just his American recruits), but 11 years later the team disbanded because of falling profits and the inability to compete with the new big-city teams that had both big-city talent and big-city payrolls.

From Major League Baseball to Major League Bust

In the late 1970s and early 1980s, two of Canada's main brewers got involved with Major League Baseball. The first was Carling O'Keefe. When the brewer purchased the promotion and broadcast rights to the Montréal Expos in 1976, it was the first time a Canadian brewer had ever sponsored professional baseball. (This move was but one of three attempts by Carling O'Keefe to endear itself to Québecois drinkers, as the brewer also sponsored the Montréal Alouettes of the CFL during the same time period and owned the Québec Nordiques hockey club.)

Labatt was the second Canadian brewer to get involved with the MLB, when, in 1976, the brewer, along with Howard Webster and the Canadian Imperial Bank of Commerce, put together an impressive pitch to land an MLB team for the city of Toronto. Labatt was successful, and their baseball team joined the American League in 1977. Labatt's 45-percent stake in the Toronto team represented the majority of the shares. As such, the brewer held a "name the team" contest and chose the "Blue Jays" as the winning team name—a name that just so happened to echo the company's most popular national brand, Labatt Blue.

In 1989, the Blue Jays moved into the new SkyDome, in which Labatt had a 48-percent stake. Two years later Labatt increased its holdings in the Blue Jays to 90 percent when the brewer purchased the shares belonging to the estate of original investor Webster. The timing of this purchase was impeccable: the Blue Jays went on to win back-to-back World Series titles in 1992 and 1993. The championship wins were even highlighted in a television commercial for Labatt Blue in the spring of 1994: a Blue beer-drinker imagined his backyard positioned exactly on the U.S.-Canadian border, where he taunted Americans with "the finest example of a true Canadian lager." To add insult to injury, he also played a tape of the Jays winning the World Series (the allusion being that not only was Canadian beer superior to American beer, but so, too, was our ball club— when baseball was supposed to be *their* sport). Too bad for Labatt that the Blue Jays were horrible in 1994, the league went on strike halfway through the season and the Canadian brewer was purchased by Interbrew in 1995. Labatt retained control of the Blue Jays, but it wasn't lost on fans that the team was no longer Canadian-owned.

In 2000, Labatt parent Interbrew sold its shares in the Blue Jays to Ted Rogers, the founder of Rogers Communications. In a separate move for the rights to the SkyDome, Labatt was outbid in the same year by Sportsco International Corporation. The corporation paid $110 million for the ballpark. Good thing for Labatt, as four years later Rogers paid only $25 million for the rights to the SkyDome. The building was originally built for just over $600 million.

Hockey Night in Canada— A Beer Love Affair

Foster Hewitt's familiar Saturday-night call to the couch has prompted hockey fans to grab a cold one and enjoy the action since the 1930s when *Hockey Night in Canada* was only aired on the radio. *HNIC* began as a national television broadcast in 1952, and within five years, the nation's most popular show had its first beer sponsor, Molson. It was with the brewer's purchase of the Canadian Arena Company (the owner of both the Montréal Canadiens and the Forum) that enabled the brewer to use its corporate ownership to become a co-sponsor with Imperial Oil of *HNIC*. (Previous to this, Molson had advertised on the radio during Canadiens games but was not an official sponsor.) The national TV broadcasts and ownership of the Montréal Canadiens not only aided Molson's profile, but it also helped with the launch of their first national brand, Molson Canadian, in 1959. The Molson sponsorship marked the beginning of what eventually became a very valuable commodity—the rights to the main hockey broadcast in Canada.

After 19 years of being a *HNIC* co-sponsor, Molson took over from Imperial Oil as the headlining sponsor in 1976. This ushered in the beginning of *Molson Hockey Night in Canada*, which lasted until rival Labatt outbid Molson for the rights to *HNIC* starting in the 1998–99 season.

Labatt celebrated its 10th season with *HNIC* and the NHL in the 2008–09 season, and with a renewed contract will be the main Canadian NHL sponsor for the next three years. The brewer's parent, AB InBev, paid $75 million to the NHL to stay on as the lead beer sponsor of the league, and in the deal, Labatt retained its Canadian sponsorship rights with *HNIC*.

DID YOU  KNOW?

The Canadian Football League is no stranger to beer sponsorship. Before its merger with Molson, Carling O'Keefe was a major player in the football league, and in 1979 the brewer purchased the Toronto Argonauts. Two years later, Carling O'Keefe made a three-year, $15.6-million sponsorship deal with the entire CFL. Twelve years after Carling O'Keefe's original purchase of the team, the Argos were famously bought by Bruce McNall, Wayne Gretzky and John Candy in 1991 (Carling itself had, by this time, sold all but five percent of its interest in the team).

Labatt, too, has a rich history in Canadian football, starting with the Winnipeg Blue Bombers, whose fans nicknamed Labatt Pilsner "Blue" because of its label's colour. The brewer eventually renamed the beer entirely to the popular "Blue." Labatt is also a long-time sponsor of the Hamilton Tiger-Cats. In an interesting twist, Molson, through its now-discount Carling brand, sponsors the Carling Zone at Tiger-Cats games, while also featuring the team on its products in the Hamilton region and holding contests for home-game tickets.

TSN: The Suds Network

Of course, "TSN" really stands for The Sports Network, but when TSN first started broadcasting, the biggest draw for viewers was the game broadcasts of the Toronto Blue Jays,

which were featured heavily on the network. It is no coincidence that TSN was the brainchild of Labatt executives Peter Widdrington and Gordon Craig. The networks' inception was in 1984, seven years after Labatt helped found the Blue Jays organization. TSN's name was originally filed with the Canadian Radio-television and Telecommunications Commission (CRTC) as the Action Canada Sports Network (ACSN) but was shortened to the snappier and simpler "TSN" by the time the channel launched. The network was originally available as a specialty offering that viewers had to pay extra for. It wasn't until 1989, the year that the original licence between the CRTC and TSN was up for renewal, that TSN became part of the basic-cable-plus package. As a result of this switch, viewer rates more than tripled during that year, with TSN watched in just over five million households before the end of 1989.

When Labatt was purchased by Interbrew in 1995, the once-Canadian-owned brewer was forced to sell off its TSN holdings to meet the CRTC's requirements surrounding Canadian ownership. The network was held in a trusteeship until a suitable buyer was found. A conglomerate of the U.S. network ESPN and Canadian heavy-hitters consisting of the Bronfman family, Gordon Craig and Reitmans Inc. purchased TSN in 1996 for $485 million—a ridiculously high return on Labatt's initial $20-million investment in the network in 1984.

TSN is currently owned by CTVglobemedia, which purchased 80 percent of the TSN holdings in 1999 when CTV was still just "CTV." The remaining 20 percent of TSN still belongs to ESPN.

I Habs to Have My Molson

As the Winnipeg Blue Bombers and the Toronto Blue Jays were synonymous with Labatt Blue, so too were the Montréal Canadiens synonymous with Molson Breweries. The Molsons were among the families who helped fund the building of the Montréal Forum, and they kept a private box in the arena beside the owners, the Raymonds. Not only did the Molsons have a hand in building what was one of the most fabled sports arenas in modern history, but it also was Hartland Molson who brought Jean Béliveau to Montréal in 1953. In a weird twist, Hartland offered Béliveau a job as a Molson public-relations representative—his job was to skate for the Canadiens and represent the brand. This before the Molsons even owned the franchise! The company purchased the legendary team from family friend Donat Raymond for $2 million in 1957. In 1964, Hartland retired from the Canadian Arena Company and passed the management of the Canadiens onto his cousin David, who, in 1968 with his brothers Peter and Billy, bought the franchise from Hartland for $3.3 million—a "family discount" of $2 million on the club's overall worth.

In a move that created a rift in the family, David and his brothers sold the Canadian Arena Company to a group led by the Bronfman family of Montréal for a profit of close to $10 million at the close of 1971. The Molsons regained ownership of the Canadiens in 1978 in what was a scramble to stop Labatt from buying the team. The Bronfmans had decided to sell, and the only offer on the table, to the tune of $20 million, was from Labatt. Before the trigger was pulled on the sale, out of loyalty to the Molsons, the Bronfmans informed the former owner of Labatt's intention to buy the hockey club. Molson immediately countered and won the team back in a deal that also included the Forum, which they had originally helped build.

Today, Molson controls a 19.9-percent stake in the team after the selling the majority of the shares and the club's new rink, the Molson Centre (now the Bell Centre), to George Gillett in 2001. As of this writing, Gillett has made it public that he is reviewing all of his holdings, and any of them, including the Canadiens, might come up for sale.

DID YOU  KNOW?

The two brewers that owned hockey clubs in Québec—Molson with the Canadiens, and Carling O'Keefe with the Québec Nordiques—sometimes took the "Battle of Québec" hockey rivalry from the ice to the boardroom. During the heated 1984 Adams Division playoff (a final that featured a Game 6 bench-clearing brawl), when then-Canadiens president Ron Corey was asked if Habs fans would switch beer companies if the Canadiens lost the series, he quipped, "The Montréal fan who has just seen his team lose doesn't want to punish himself twice." The Habs triumphed in Game 6, eliminating the Nordiques from the playoffs. Québec had its revenge the next season in an Adams Division finals rematch, taking the series in seven games.

 Molson is the official beer supplier of the 2010 Vancouver Winter Olympic Games.

RED-CARPET SUDS

The Famous Case of the Right Place at the Right Time

The discovery of Pamela Anderson wasn't as cut and dried as being in the right place at the right time. As Paul Brent discloses in his book *Lager Heads*, Anderson wasn't just a stunning BC Lions fan who happened have on a Labatt Blue Zone crop top that was shown on the big screen at a football game. The reality of the situation was that Anderson was living with a friend, Jamie Moberg, in 1989. He was a sales representative for Labatt, who had just launched their "Blue Zone" campaign, which was targeted at college-age kids. Moberg decked out Anderson in tailored Blue Zone gear and the pair headed to a Lions game. As Moberg remembers, the duo moved several times to different prime fan-shooting areas of the stadium with the hope of getting Anderson on the big screen—to advertise Blue Zone. Finally, she was shown to the crowd, and the legend was born. As for reports that Anderson then went down to centre field and was introduced to the crowd, Brent and Moberg never make mention of any such occurrence, and Anderson's official website doesn't say anything about BC, let alone the BC Lions.

After the big-screen stunt, Moberg and Anderson had some posters made up of her in the Blue Zone shirt. Moberg pitched to his superiors the idea of Anderson being a model for the campaign. Labatt wasn't interested—that is, until Anderson and a photo used for Moberg's poster ended up in *Playboy* in 1990. Labatt, Moberg later jests, "purchased 10,000 copies of that poster."

Teen Wolf Likes Canadian Suds

Remember that scene in *Teen Wolf* where Michael J. Fox, playing mild-mannered teenager Scott Howard, is out with his best friend, Rupert "Stiles" Stilinski, and the pair are on their way to a house party? The duo, obviously underage, head to a liquor store with the plan of purchasing a keg for the party. Scott nervously attempts to order a keg from the old man running the liquor store, but he won't play ball. A rebuffed Scott, angry, repeats his request, this time in his wolf voice while flashing his red wolf eyes. The clerk, freaked out, obliges, and Scott calmly returns to being a regular teenager—ordering a pack of licorice to make everything seem all the more casual. But then, to Scott and Stiles' dismay, they show up at the party to find a surplus of kegs already there.

In real life, Fox isn't a werewolf, nor does he like American beer—and why should he? He is Canadian, after all. The native of Edmonton, Alberta, has a fondness for East Coast suds, as he revealed to Jay Leno on the *Tonight Show*. Fox stated he prefers to drink Moosehead Ale when he can. After the show aired, Moosehead surprised Fox by sending a truck to the star's home with several cases of his favourite beer. Although Fox described one his favourite brews as "Moosehead Ale," a name Moosehead beer doesn't technically have (they do have a Pale Ale), I'll let him slide on his misstep. Come on, he was Marty McFly!

Canadian Bacon

Director Michael Moore's only fiction film, *Canadian Bacon* (1995), starring John Candy, is about the U.S. government's search for a new enemy given that the Cold War is over. Through media manipulation, the government attempts to create an enemy out of Canada. Candy's character, Sheriff Bud B. Boomer, who lives on the American side of the Niagara Falls border, takes the matter into his own hands.

Bud's hatred for Canada is ignited at a brawl during a hockey game between a U.S. team facing off against a Canadian home team. As Canada is filling the net, Bud and his American friends complain about Canada (and how the nation cheats at baseball to win the World Series). But it is Bud's line, "I'll tell you another thing, their [Canadian] beer sucks," that stops everything dead in its tracks. The captain of the Canadian team jumps over the boards to attack Bud, and all hell breaks loose. Time and time again Moore has proven that no one in Hollywood understands the Canadian psyche as well as he does.

It Wouldn't be a Canadian Beer Book Without…

…Bob and Doug McKenzie. That would be like winter without snow or beer without…doughnuts? The *SCTV* duo (Rick Moranis and Dave Thomas), who made it to the big screen in *The Adventures of Bob & Doug McKenzie: Strange Brew* (1983), have been busy in the last 10 years. The hosers were featured in Molson ads in the U.S. in the late 1990s to help boost sales of Molson Golden, Molson Canadian, Molson Light and Molson Ice. In 2003, the pair was tapped as the voices of the animated moose brothers in the Disney film *Brother Bear*, and in 2007, Brick Brewing released limited-edition Red Cap bottles and cases featuring the bumbling, beer-loving siblings. Now the brew-chasing brothers are in an animated TV show: *The Animated Adventures of Bob & Doug McKenzie* premiered April 2009 on Global. The

show was created by the Van Nuys-based animation company Animax, owned by Thomas. If you have noticed something off in the show, though, you aren't wrong; Bob, traditionally played by Moranis, is voiced by *Full House* alumnus and fellow Canadian, Dave Coulier. Moranis is a producer on *The Animated Adventures* but was not up for having to tape so many episodes in California, away from his New York home.

Either way, I'm glad to have the hosers back!

Ka-roo-koo-koo-ka-koo-koo-koo!

CONCLUSION

I always get asked "What's your favourite beer?" and I always give the same answer—"depends on the season"—because as I have gotten older, the craft-brewing scene in Canada has only grown, providing me with a bigger and better selection of brew. How can I have a favourite?! Consequently (and because of my slight maturation from the days of attempting to chug American lagers by the kitchen sink), having a favourite beer or beer company isn't such a big deal—what's important to me now is simply having the option to drink a great-tasting, natural, Canadian product. Of course I have my standby lagers and ales that I fall back on when I can't make up my mind or just feel like drinking something familiar, but now more than ever I relish trying new brews and exploring what the independent craft brewers of our country are creating.

That being said, readers should know that drinking big-market beer is perfectly fine, too—the goal here is to broaden your horizons, not chastise your choices. Sure, some craft purists will turn up their noses at the very idea of consuming a Molson Canadian or a Labatt Blue, but beer is a celebration, and while the majority of big-market brews are often low in flavour and high in adjunct ingredients, those beers are still part of the celebration, and without them we wouldn't have the craft resurgence our country is currently experiencing. Besides, I enjoy a Labatt 50 every once in a while and, admittedly, have had a lot of fun at its expense.

I like to think of mainstream lagers and ales as the gateway brews to the craft-beer segment, and it is my hope that this book was able to serve you as another type of entry into the exploration of Canada's beer culture. What is represented on these pages is just the tip of the Canadian beer iceberg, so get out there and drink it in. And what better way to experience beer than through the pint glass?

Cheers!

ABOUT THE AUTHOR

Steve Cameron

Born and raised in small-town Ontario, most of Steve Cameron's adult life has been spent trying to get to know beer better. He took his first sip at 16 from a wide-mouthed, squat bottle of Mickey's lager and then promptly ran to the sink to spit it out. But Steve wanted to love beer, so he slowly introduced himself to it, starting with Boomerang lemon malt and working his way to Moosehead, his first true favourite. Now Steve alternates beers with the season, preferring pumpkin ales in the fall and wheat beers in the summer. An avid sports fan and hockey player, Steve maintains there is nothing quite as refreshing after physical exertion as a good, crisp lager. He currently lives in Toronto with his girlfriend and plans to begin experimenting with his own homemade brews soon.

ABOUT THE ILLUSTRATORS

Djordje Todorovic

Djordje Todorovic is an artist/illustrator living in Toronto, Ontario. He first moved to the city to go to York University to study fine arts. It was there that he got a taste for illustrating while working as the illustrator for his college paper *Mondo Magazine*. He has since worked on various projects and continues to perfect his craft. Aside from his artistic work, Djordje devotes his time volunteering at the Print and Drawing Centre at the Art Gallery of Ontario. When he is not doing that he is out trotting the globe.

ABOUT THE ILLUSTRATORS

Peter Tyler

Peter is a graduate of the Vancouver Film School's Visual Art and Design and Classical animation programs. Though his ultimate passion is in film-making, he is also intent on developing his draftsmanship and storytelling, with the aim of using those skills in future filmic misadventures.

Roger Garcia

Roger Garcia is a self-taught artist with some formal training who specializes in cartooning and illustration. He is an immigrant from El Salvador, and during the last few years, his work has been primarily cartoons and editorial illustrations in pen and ink. Recently he has started painting once more. Focusing on simplifying the human form, he uses a bright minimal palette and as few elements as possible. His work can be seen in newspapers, magazines, promo material and on www.rogergarcia.ca